Delffse Porceleyne

Delffse Porceleyne

Dutch delftware 1620-1850

Jan Daniël van Dam

Waanders Publishers

Rijksmuseum, Amsterdam

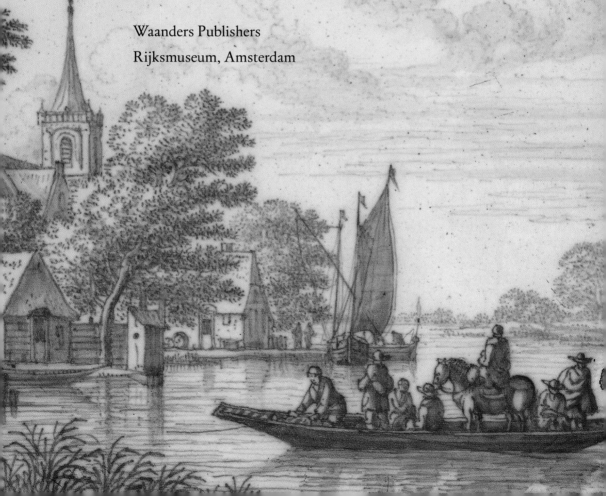

Exclusive sponsor
Aronson Antiquairs
Since 1881
Nieuwe Spiegelstraat 39
P.O. Box 15556
NL-1001 NB Amsterdam
Tel. +31 20 - 623 3103
Fax +31 20 - 638 3066
e-mail: aronson@aronson.nl
web: www.DutchDelftware.com
'Specialists in 17th- and
18th-century Dutch delftware'

Contents

Inside front jacket flap: map of the Netherlands showing the towns and villages mentioned in the book
Inside back jacket flap: map of Delft showing the potteries referred to in the book

Foreword

Delft faience is among the greatest Dutch achievements of the 17th and 18th centuries. Over the last hundred and fifty years a great many private individuals and museums, in the Netherlands and beyond, have amassed collections of delftware. It is almost self-evident that the most important collection of this 'national' product in the Netherlands should be in the Rijksmuseum – a leading position that was not, however, acquired until 1916. The gift presented by the children of James Loudon meant that the collection put together between 1868 and 1876 by their uncle, John Loudon, could be added to the museum collection in its entirety. Just how important this nucleus of pieces still is to the Rijksmuseum's delftware collection can be seen from the selection that the senior curator of ceramics made for this book, which has been produced in association with Waanders Publishers. Even now, after more than eighty years of active collecting and additions to the collection, almost half of the hundred and fifty items illustrated come from the Loudon Collection.

Seventy-five years ago the Berlin publisher Richard Schmidt & Co. asked the then senior curator of the Rijksmuseum, Ferrand Hudig, to write a handbook on Dutch delftware. The Rijksmuseum's collection served to illustrate a well-crafted art historical account. The fact that the collection has again served as the basis for a general book about Delft faience is very pleasing.

We are particularly indebted to Aronson Antiquairs of Amsterdam, specialists in delftware, whose generous contribution made it possible to print all the illustrations in colour.

We learn from the last chapter in the book that by about 1850 interest in Delft faience had effectively vanished in the Netherlands. An exhibition in Delft in 1863 attracted a great deal of attention and this, coupled with a growing interest in the past, opened the eyes of a new group of buyers. Since then delftware has been widely collected and the subject of serious study. The present book is a response to this enthusiasm, which is still very much alive a century and a half later.

Ronald de Leeuw
Director General

A double prelude
(1600-1647)

Significant political and economic changes took place in the Netherlands during the first twenty years of the Eighty Years' War (1568-1648). This protracted revolt started as a conflict about money and religion between local nobles and cities on one side, and the central authority in Brussels, governing in the name of the King of Spain, on the other. Although it had not been the intention, the revolt escalated into a war of independence. This ultimately led to the partition of the Netherlands into a Roman Catholic southern part, which remained loyal to the Spanish Crown, and a Protestant northern part, which became a republic. In the original Netherlands of seventeen provinces, the southern provinces of Brabant and Flanders, with Brussels and Antwerp as the principal cities, were economically stronger. After 1585, however, economic power shifted to the northern province of Holland, where Amsterdam was the most important city. The theatre of war had moved to the eastern and southern part of the present-day Netherlands, allowing the economy of the province of Holland, in particular, to develop in peace. The province rapidly became very prosperous. This had a significant impact on the increasing use of luxury goods of all kinds, and hence on their manufacture. An industry producing earthenware items finished with painted tin glaze – known as majolica – benefited greatly from this trend. Around 1600, good quality majolica ware and tiles were being made in the prosperous north, in cities like Haarlem, Amsterdam, Rotterdam and Delft. Output was limited at first, largely confined to apothecary wares – ointment pots and syrup jugs – and tiles, indispensable as wall covering and decoration in Dutch interiors. After 1600, the focus increasingly shifted on to plates, dishes and tiles, while apothecary jars, drinking vessels and similar goods took a back seat. It was the new products that offered consumers a wider choice, proving a welcome replacement for often primitive utensils like wooden plates (or trenchers as they were known).

Immigrants were also an important factor in the growth of the majolica industry. Most of them were Protestants fleeing from the war and the religious persecution in the south, who brought their working methods and

Between 1960 and 1990 many Dutch inner cities were redeveloped to meet modern housing needs. The demolition of large numbers of 17th-century houses revealed cesspits containing tens of thousands of shards of broken pottery. This material threw new light on the earliest period of Delft faience.

Nicolaes Maes, *Woman plucking a duck*, c. 1655-1656. Philadelphia Museum of Art.

The woman concentrates on plucking a duck while a cat creeps up on a second bird lying on the ground. There are various items of lead-glazed earthenware to hand, among them a dish decorated with a landscape and with a border derived from Chinese porcelain.

A short passage in the margin of Adriaen Bogaert's inventory, Haarlem 1568, producer of majolica:
Inventory of the goods found in the house of Adriaen Bogaert, pottery maker by the Great Bridge, drawn up by the bailiff of Haarlem and the royal commissioners for Kennemerland, on the last day of March in the year 1568 and the same on the 9th of April thereafter, valued by Maritgen Bartelmeeusdochter and Els in den Salm, second-hand dealers of the said Town, in pounds and shillings of 40 groats: … 54 dozen butter dishes, at 5 s the dozen; 12 dozen pint and half-pint jugs, at 12 s the dozen; 300 saucers and small pots, at 8 s the hundred …, 2 kilns of unfired earthenware, valued with all the tools used in pottery, 8 g in total. A few lines from the inventory of what would have been a pottery's standard stock at this time. But also: *In the anteroom: 23 wooden trenchers.* For their own use, Adriaen Bogaert's family still had twenty-three wooden plates!

their technical expertise to the north. The painted decoration of the majolica ware and the tiles was entirely in the Italian-Antwerp style, as practised in Antwerp. Pieces were decorated with simplified foliage, an ornamental design of, for instance, a rosette or a stylized star or, just occasionally, a figurative decoration that was usually borrowed from a print.

The customary process, when a new product is developed in a prosperous country, is that the product starts out by being coarse and primitive, and can only be afforded by the very rich. Little by little it is refined and improved, and a varied range in different price brackets means that it also comes within the reach of other sectors of the population. In the case of majolica, this process was already well under way prior to 1600, but it was disrupted shortly after the turn of the century as far as the largest category, the plates and the dishes, was concerned. The reason lay with the Dutch East India Company, the trading company which in 1602 obtained the sole right in the Netherlands to trade with and in Asia. The company became immensely successful. In 1602, the Dutch East India Company started to bring Chinese porcelain to the Netherlands. At first the quantities were modest, but after about 1610 the volume increased year on year. By 1620, East Indiamen were bringing in around 100,000 pieces a year, all destined, it should be noted, for a wealthy group among the Dutch population that certainly numbered no more than 250,000 people. These imports of porcelain forced the manufacturers of majolica and tiles to make a choice, faced as they were with

immense competition from the popular, wafer-thin porcelain. A further problem was that they were unable to copy these porcelain wares because the type of clay that was required and the manufacturing process involved were unknown in Europe, and were to remain so until the early part of the 18th century.

Some majolica makers simply gave up and closed their potteries around 1620. Others concentrated on the product that was not affected by the Chinese imports: wall tiles. A third group elected to produce a cheap product by making the designs coarser and decorating them more crudely. They were aiming at a different sector of the market, lower down the social scale. After 1630 this sector was made up primarily of the prosperous rural areas in the provinces of Holland, Zeeland and Friesland and the areas to which the Netherlands exported goods: in Northern Germany, Scandinavia, Flanders, Northern France, the French coast as far as Bordeaux and probably England. These dishes and plates, until about 1680 painted with coarse but powerful decoration often similar to the designs used on tiles, occupy a specific place in the overall range of tin-glazed earthenware. A small number of firms continued to make dishes like this in later years; the wares became ever cruder and the decoration increasingly primitive, as they moved steadily down the social scale. Eventually, by the late 19th century, majolica ware had found its way on to the tables of the peasants scraping a living on the poor sandy soil in the east of the Netherlands and the adjacent areas of Germany.

Of the millions of dishes that must have been produced in the 1625-1650 period, only a very few survive. The decorations were taken from various sources. The woman with a yoke and two milk pails dating from 1630 (fig. 1) could well have appeared on a wall tile of the same period, and the angel blowing a trumpet (fig. 2) would not have been out of place on an Italian dish. The painting around the rim of this dish, however, is derived from Chinese porcelain. The decorations were contemporary and without doubt catered to the tastes of a rather unsophisticated public. The people who designed these decorations were certainly not innovators, they simply followed the trend.

A fourth group of manufacturers, finally, tried to refine the product and its decoration, endeavouring to get as close to the imported porcelain as they could. They wanted to match the thinness of the body, the clarity and sheen of the glaze, the colour and the fine brushwork of the exotic ware from China. And this meant that they had to find solutions to numerous technical problems. When dishes were made thinner, they often warped while they were drying. When the lead glaze on the back of plates was replaced with tin glaze, both sides of the object remained mat. Efforts at product

1

Dish, dated 1630, diam. 24 cm.

The woman carrying a yoke and two milk pails would certainly not have been out of place on a tile. At this period, dishes and wall tiles were produced in the same potteries.

2

Dish, c. 1630-1650, diam. 33 cm.

The angel blowing a trumpet has stepped straight off an Italian dish from Faenza; the painter borrowed the border from imported Chinese porcelain. People in the 17th century were not unduly concerned about plagiarism or imitation.

development and the technical improvements they entailed eventually led to the addition to the indigenous clays of a type of clay not found in the Netherlands. This was marl, a clay with a high lime content, which was imported from Doornik (Tournai) in the Southern Netherlands, and sometimes, in the early years, from Norwich in East Anglia.

The new, finer product was thrown on a mould – usually made of plaster but occasionally of wood or stone –, fired, and covered all over with a white, opaque tin glaze. After a piece had been painted it was fired again in a cylindrical container, known as a saggar. Saggars were made of a fire-resistant loam, a type of clay, which was reinforced with finely ground pot-

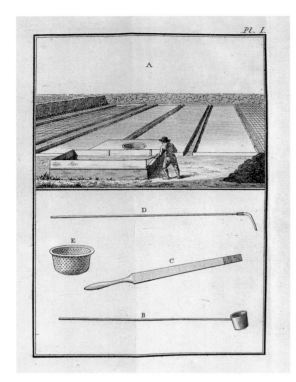

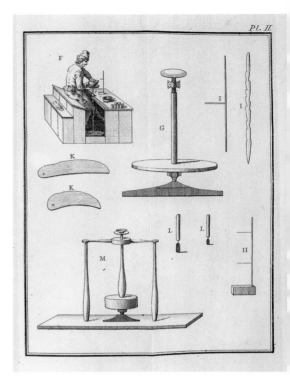

Four of the five engravings in the little book entitled *De Plateelbakker of Delftsch aardewerkmaaker* by Gerrit Paape with the description of the production process and the original 'explanations'.

Plate I
A. The Clay Washer
B. The Bucket
C. The Spade
D. The Draw Knife
E. The Sieve

sherds. Each plate rested on three or four ceramic pegs pushed through the wall of the saggar. The visible scars on the front of the dish caused by the use of rough ceramic triangular spacers to separate the dishes when they were stacked in the kiln became a thing of the past: the marks caused by the pegs were now on the back of the piece. Finally, the inside of the saggar had to be saturated with undiluted lead glaze, and carefully sealed with clay so as to ensure that the component of the glaze which gives the shine could not evaporate during firing nor be absorbed by the saggar.

Earthenware of this kind is also known as faience, but the product that was developed between 1618 and 1624 in Delft became known in English as delftware. In 17th-century Holland, it was referred to as 'Dutch porcelain'. The technical development of this 'Dutch porcelain' was concentrated in two factories, which acquired names reflecting their products during the course of the 17th century: De Porceleyne Schotel (The Porcelain Dish), owned by Elisabeth Cornelisdr Suycker and her second husband Hendrick Marcelisz van Gogh, and De Porceleyne Lampetkan (The Porcelain Ewer), owned by Cornelis Harmansz Valckenhoven.

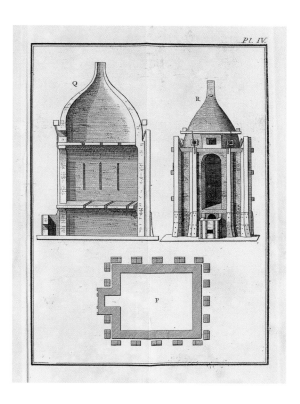

The most important character in the story was perhaps the manager of De Porceleyne Schotel, Willem Jansz Verstraeten. On 24 December 1617, the owners of the business signed a contract with him 'to disclose, without concealing anything, all his skills and practices, which he has and shall know, concerning the aforesaid making of pottery, without being permitted to teach the same to anyone else'. This contract was renewed in 1623, and in January 1625 Verstraeten and the owners executed a deed before a notary, stating that they would apply for a patent on the pottery-making method that he had taught the other two. This never happened, because in the same year, having given all his skills and inventiveness to the company for the best part of a decade, Verstraeten set up his own pottery in Haarlem. This technical development was so new and at the same time so thoroughgoing that a multiplicity of sizes, shapes, standards and working practices was established in the potteries in the second quarter of the 17th century, and these were to remain unchanged until the wholesale collapse of the industry in Delft in about 1850. The majority of the wares produced by De Porceleyne Schotel and De Porceleyne Lampetkan were small plates,

approximately 20 centimetres in diameter, with a finely-painted border and a very varied range of decorative motifs in the centre (fig. 3), which, although these potteries certainly did not make tiles any longer, were often very reminiscent of the tile designs of the time. They evidently had a stock of perforated design stencils for tiles, which they continued to use for the new product for reasons of economy or convenience.

Around 1625 fashion as a whole underwent a change and there was a general move away from bright colours. Dress became less elaborate and predominantly black. Painters like Rembrandt and Jan van Goyen started to use muted palettes. This universal trend

3
Small plate, c. 1625-1650, diam. 19.8 cm.

In inventories, items like this are listed as butter dishes; they were the small plates used for thick slices of buttered bread.

Jan Steen, *The doctor's visit*. Mauritshuis, The Hague.

Jan Steen had a small jug made by De Porceleyne Schotel as a studio prop. Objects that were not imported from China, like these little jugs, were nonetheless decorated with Chinese scenes.

4

Ointment pot, c. 1625-1650,
h. 9.6 cm, diam. 14.2 cm.

The painting of the earthenware
items used by apothecaries
followed the urban fashion of
simple decorations painted in
blue.

The names that had been given
to the saggars in the middle of
the 17th century on the basis
of the objects that were fired in
them were still used even when
those particular objects had not
been made for years: Paape in
1794: *There are yet other sorts of
saggars, like* Twijfelaars *and*
Saucier *saggars, in which they
fire large and small butter dishes:*
Kloekkarel *saggars, which are
filled with the so-called* Kenen-
burgers, *or hollow Drinking
vessels, small Bowls, Coffee dishes
etc.*

obviously also influenced the decoration on majolica, tiles and the newly
developed faience from Delft. At that
time changes like this occurred more
gradually and took much longer to per-
colate down to all levels of society than
they do today. After 1625, earthenware
pieces for the wealthy were painted in
just one colour, blue. It was chosen
because it is a neutral colour that set
off the sober fashions. Blue was also an
easy colour when it came to firing the
glaze: there was very little that could
go wrong and the decoration seldom
ran. The choice of the colour was also
undoubtedly influenced by the blue-
painted, imported Chinese porcelain.
In other sectors of society, though,
colourfully painted utensils retained
their popularity for a very long time.
This was certainly true of the well-to-
do farming communities in the rural
areas of Holland, Zeeland and Friesland. It is not impossible that the manufacturers of majolica dishes (figs. 1
and 2) sought their markets in these
regions. But whenever anyone with

aspirations to urban style ordered
majolica, because the pieces in question were not available either in
imported Chinese porcelain or in
faience, these objects were as a matter
of course painted in blue. The ointment jar (fig. 4) is good example of
this. The apothecary ordered robustly
thrown pots, decorated with a blue
painted pattern that is similar to the
designs on the rims of the popular little breakfast plates that the two leading
Delft potteries, De Porceleyne Schotel
and De Porceleyne Lampetkan, were
producing in their tens of thousands.
All manufacturers, however, whether
they were producing old-fashioned
majolica or faience, obeyed one cardi-
nal rule: before 1620 all pieces, both
plates and dishes, had a smoothly curv-
ing back, as had been customary in
Italian dishes. All the pieces produced
after about 1625 have a profile with a
distinct kink, a shape borrowed from
Chinese porcelain. Various other models were also developed during this
period – jugs and tankards, and dishes
with coarsely and finely fluted rim and
foot. The shapes of the hollow-ware
were often derived from stoneware jugs
imported from the west of Germany,
the most common drinking vessel at
the time; the shapes of the flat-ware
were based on metal plates and dishes.

In 1642, after seventeen years in business in Haarlem, Willem Verstraeten
suffered a stroke that left him an
invalid, and he turned his pottery over
to his son Gerrit. Old Willem made
such a good recovery, however, that he
set up a new firm in the same year, with
an agreement that the son would make
the new-fangled faience and the father
would confine himself to the produc-

tion of old-fashioned majolica. With a view to safeguarding his position in the Dutch market, Gerrit entered into a restraint of trade agreement with the two Delft manufacturers, Hendrick van Gogh of De Porceleyne Schotel and Ermpgen Cornelisdr, widow of Cornelis Valckenhoven of De Porceleyne Lampetkan. All three were described as 'Dutch porcelain makers'. They agreed that they would all pay their workers the same wages and that, without prior consent, they would not poach one another's employees on pain of a fine of 100 guilders. It can be seen from this that these firms made the same product – 'Dutch porcelain' – and that they had such a dominant position in the Netherlands that as far as their workers were concerned they did not have to fear any outside competition. They can be regarded as the market leaders. It can also be deduced from this important document that there was a shortage of skilled and qualified workers.

A war in China meant that imports of Chinese porcelain into the Netherlands, which had risen to something in the order of 250,000 pieces a year, declined between 1644 and 1647, and were to come to an almost complete standstill over the next five years. Seeing this gap in the market, the owners of the only two potteries producing faience in Delft seized their opportunity. They started to make faience on a large scale with decoration in the Chinese style.

In the autumn of 1647, it dawned on Willem Verstraeten, in the final analysis one of the most experienced earthenware manufacturers in the Nether-

lands, that he had backed the wrong horse when he signed the contract with his son Gerrit in 1642. He wanted to switch from old-fashioned majolica to faience and, from January 1648 onwards, tried in a less than dignified way to get out of the agreement with his son. The ensuing legal proceedings centred on the question of precisely what 'Dutch porcelain' was, with the father focusing on the decoration and the son on the material.

After a few skirmishes, Willem Verstraeten brought the big guns to bear on his son, and got the cream of the Delft 'Dutch porcelain makers' to testify. On 26 February, Hendrick van Gogh testified that 'he knew in truth that everything that is called porcelain (and is made here) that the same must be painted all over, and that what was painted with little wreaths or with little manikins or with coats of arms, that the same was called white goods'. The same day two other Delft potters gave similar testimony. The three men stated that white goods were faience with a small amount of decoration and that 'porcelain' was faience with full decoration. The last two statements on the father's behalf only speak to the decoration, whereas the son evidently asserted that all the better made flatware (in other words faience) was called 'Dutch porcelain', irrespective of the decoration. The allotment in the contract will almost certainly also have been based on the material and not on the decoration. As far as competition was concerned, there would have been absolutely no point in producing faience with Chinese decoration before 1647, because up to that date the demand for top-quality ceramics with Chinese decoration was after

5
Dish, c. 1650-1660,
diam. 31.1 cm.

A notorious lawsuit made it
impossible for one potter in
Haarlem, Willem Verstraeten, to
decorate his wares with Chinese
designs. He was consequently
compelled to fall back on Italian
examples, which he combined
with Dutch landscapes or, as
in this case, a magnificently
executed coat of arms.

all entirely satisfied by imported Chinese porcelain. In the first twenty-five
years, 'Dutch porcelain' was indeed just
faience with non-Chinese decoration.
Be this as it may, on 30 April 1648
the father dismissed all his workers
and sent them to work for his children
Gysbert and Maria, who were still
minors. Everything indicates that the
father was in the wrong and that the
statements given by his business asso-
ciates served only to muddy the waters
still further. There was a whole series

of controversial legal cases between
father and son, involving numerous
witness statements by colleagues and
workers from Haarlem, Leiden, Delft,
Amsterdam and elsewhere. These give
us a good insight into who was important in the earthenware sector and
how the manufacture and the sale of
the products in the Netherlands were
organized. One witness statement
clearly reveals the direction in which
the father was forced to go. Meeus
Jansz Goris, 'delftware merchant of

6
Dish, c. 1650-1660,
diam. 39.5 cm.

The print used as the model
is higher than it is wide
(c. 28 x 20 cm), so some
shrubs were added on the left
and some buildings put in on
the right to fit the symmetri-
cal round surface of the dish,
which is almost 40 centimetres
in diameter.

Monnikendam' stated that he 'appraises
es and judges such type of earthenware
as Willem Jansz is presently producing, to wit dishes bearing coats of arms
and similar, as not being porcelain …
for six months he has bought from
the plaintiff such type as he presently
makes, … that it is a new invention'
and the ruling of the Court of Holland
handed down in the autumn of 1650
to the effect that the father could produce wares with 'new inventions, however not in the manner of porcelain'.
The last judgment, that of the High
Court, is not known; possibly a set-
tlement was reached in the end. It
appears that the father continued to
make faience, but after he had said
during the court cases that Chinese
decoration was the main characteristic
of 'Dutch porcelain', he had to refrain
from that type of painting, and for the
first few years after the legal proceedings he could not possibly have pro-

duced faience with a Chinese design
on it. A group of faience ware bearing
designs that departed from the current
patterns was consequently created
in his pottery during this period –
designs described as 'new inventions'
by Meeus Goris, 'delftware merchant
of Monnikendam', in his witness
statement for Willem Verstraeten.
This is the faience of the mid-17th century with decorations after examples
from the Italian city of Urbino, like
the fine dish (fig. 5), in which an Italian
inspired rim is combined with a blazon
with five fleur de lis and a complete
painted coat of arms. Dishes with
coats of arms had been a specialty of
Verstraeten's majolica pottery in the
1640s. But Willem had still more up
his sleeve both technically and artistically. The dish with the depiction of
Abraham's Sacrifice (fig. 6) is a magnificent example of what this Haarlem
firm was capable of in 1650 and the
years that followed: refined painting
that has remained perfectly sharp and
stable during the firing process. Not
a line has run or become blurred and
all the nuances in the blue have been
retained. Verstraeten undoubtedly
bought a number of prints to aid in the
design and production of this piece.

6A
This print by Egbert van
Panderen after P. de Jode of
Abraham's Sacrifice was used
as a model for the dish on
the left, which was made in
Willem Verstraeten's pottery
in Haarlem.

7
Dish, dated 1654, diam. 38 cm.

A dish bearing the portrait of
Frederick Henry, Prince of
Orange, seven years after his
death, was undoubtedly made to
order. The painter used a print
by Van Meurs after a painting
by the Utrecht artist and court
painter Gerard van Honthorst.

The dish dated 1654 (fig. 7) must have
had a political significance: Frederick
Henry had died in 1647, and between
1651 and 1672 power politics kept the
post of stadholder unfilled.
After 1650, when there were still no
imports of oriental porcelain from
China, the outcome of the court case
began to carry less weight and old
Willem's pottery in Haarlem did produce faience with Chinese decoration.

The decoration on this dish (fig. 8),
though, is no slavish copy of Chinese
porcelain like those that the Delft potters generally made in the early years.
It is a free, more individual interpretation, which can rightly be counted
among the earliest examples of Dutch
chinoiserie.
Willem Verstraeten died in 1655, followed two years later by his son Gerrit.
Gerrit's widow sold the house in the

8
Dish, c. 1650-1660,
diam. 37.5 cm.

The decoration is not a copy
taken directly from a Chinese
porcelain dish. It is an invented
landscape executed in the
Chinese manner.

Begijnhof in 1663; the deeds of sale
make no mention of a faience pottery.
Willem's pottery was passed on to a
servant, Jacob Pietersz 't Kind. In 1670
he was still listed as a majolica maker,
but in 1682 the property in the
Spaarnewouderstraat was sold.

As well as the simple painted majolica
dishes, polychrome painted faience was
produced on a limited scale for the customers in the rural areas and probably also for export. These buyers were
evidently not yet ready for the blue
painted faience with its generally much
more refined decoration. It is impossible to estimate the extent of the output
of unpainted white goods and these
simply decorated and relatively brightly
coloured utensils. Virtually none of it
has survived, and what there is, is not
usually included in the large, official

9

Puzzle jug, c. 1650-1670,
h. 16 cm.

Puzzle jugs were a feature of the
far from refined bouts of eating
and drinking for which the
Netherlands was notorious
throughout Europe in the 16th
and 17th centuries. With the
nipple on the edge in his mouth,
a drinker could suck the contents of the jug out through the
hollow handle.

and highly visible collections of Delft
earthenware. The puzzle jug (fig. 9)
dating from the third quarter of the
17th century is a joke item, typical of
this period. If someone tries to drink
from the vessel without knowing the
trick of it, the contents will pour all
over his lap. The two small plates
(fig. 10) dating from 1683, were without doubt used in a tavern. One text
speaks up in defence of the landlord,

the other of the landlady; it apparently
never entered the rhymester's head that
they could both be hospitable and
agreeable.

10
Two small plates, dated 1683, diam. 21.5 and 21 cm.

Small plates measuring around 20 centimetres in diameter, known as 'butter dishes', must have been part of every household inventory. Six- or twelve-line rhymes to stimulate the appetite were among the standard decorations. The rhyme was usually split up over a set of six plates.

Allow a quiet man
doing what he can
the pleasures of the table
what avail soft words
and a friendly reception
if the wife is a sour creature

A Quiet wife
and her labours
delight the table
but if the host
sulks and growls
all is wrong

A glorious success:
mass product and rarity
(1647-1680)

The Treaty of Westphalia, signed in the German city of Munster in 1648, marked the end of the war between the Netherlands and Spain. The Netherlands was recognized as a union of seven provinces acting together as a republic. Peace also returned elsewhere in Europe. Many of the German states had been devastated by the Thirty Years' War (1618-1648), a wide-ranging religious and political power struggle. These states were trying to recover from the immense damage caused by this war, which also ended with a treaty signed in Munster in 1648. The people of the Southern Netherlands, which had remained in the hands of the King of Spain, had reconciled themselves to the partition from the northern part and focused on their own territory. After years of religious disputes, France was about to enter a period of expansion under Louis XIV.

The Republic of the United Provinces, as the Netherlands was officially known, was unquestionably a phenomenon amidst all the monarchies in Europe – not only because it was a state without a king, but also because in the second half of the 17th century the Nether-

lands was an economic and political force to be reckoned with, a small country but a major power. Political policy was governed to a significant extent by the desire to promote and protect free foreign trade. The two wars with England (1652-1654 and 1665-1667) were in a sense trade wars; there was absolutely no intention of expanding the territory of the Netherlands. These wars were fought primarily at sea, and although people in the Netherlands were certainly very concerned, they were not directly inconvenienced by them. The worst that they had to endure was that overseas imports of luxury items – goods like spices and porcelain from the Orient, wine and salt from France and Portugal – were hindered during the war years.

The Netherlands was well off in this period, but the steady growth in prosperity that had continued uninterrupted for the previous seventy years was over. Thanks in part to the amassed wealth and the technical and economic advantage that the Netherlands had over the other countries of Europe, the average per capita income was to remain the highest in

Large vases used to decorate the 'Salon', the principal room in a house.

27

Europe for a very long time to come. The difference between rich and poor was also much smaller in the Netherlands than it was elsewhere. In consequence, there was a very large, well-to-do middle class that could afford all sorts of luxuries, a unique phenomenon in Europe.

The economic situation in the Dutch countryside was diverse. The hundred years between 1650 and 1750 were a period of stagnation and crises for rural areas, although the picture did vary from region to region at different times. The growth of arable and livestock farming stagnated between 1650 and 1675, and this situation worsened between 1675 and 1690. After 1690 there was a temporary upturn in the agricultural economy. The farmers in North Holland and Friesland suffered greater hardship during the farming crises than did, for instance, the farmers on the South Holland and Zeeland islands, who earned a proportion of their living from industrial crops like madder, which was used to make red dye.

In 1644 a war broke out in China which, although it was so far away, had far-reaching implications for the import of Chinese porcelain into the Netherlands and for Dutch earthenware manufacture.

The war started when the Manchus, a people that lived to the north of China, succeeded in capturing the country from the Ming dynasty. They made Beijing their capital, but had great difficulty establishing their authority in the Southern Chinese coastal provinces. Zheng Chenggong (1623-1662), a warlord loyal to the Ming dynasty who became known in

the west as Koxinga, a corrupted form of the name (in fact the Dutch romanization of his popular name 'lord of the royal surname'), emerged as a rebel leader and successfully resisted the Manchus for many years.

The war was disastrous for the manufacture and export of porcelain. Between 1644 and 1647 the volume of imports into the Netherlands fell from more than 200,000 to around 125,000 pieces a year. Very little archive material about porcelain imports covering the years 1648 to 1654 has survived, but in 1654 imports amounted to a mere 15,000 items; in the next two years they had essentially dried up. 1657 marked the start of a total standstill of official exports of Chinese porcelain to the Netherlands that was to continue for thirty years. In 1662 Koxinga captured Formosa (the present-day Taiwan), until then a Dutch possession. The Dutch East India Company had used this island off the coast of China as an entrepôt – among other things for porcelain.

In 1647, when porcelain imports had fallen to almost half, the reports about the war in China and the sharp reduction in imports of porcelain to the Netherlands must have been more or less general knowledge. It must have been clear not just to the East India Company but to the Dutch faience and majolica potteries that this was no temporary dip and that a new era was dawning.

The East India Company was not beaten this easily, however, and went to extreme lengths to preserve the lucrative porcelain trade. In July 1652 Jan van Riebeeck, founder of the Company's staging post, the Cape of Good Hope in South Africa, sent a sample of white-firing clay from the Cape to Batavia, the Company's administrative centre in Asia, to see whether it could be used to make porcelain. It could not. After 1652, small quantities of imitation porcelain from Persia were sent to Batavia. The crude Persian wares may have been suitable for sectors of the Asian market, but they certainly would not do for the discerning Dutch consumer.

Porcelain had been made on a small scale in Japan since the early 17th century. The Dutch East India Company tried to make good the lost trade by importing Japanese porcelain painted in the Chinese style. Efforts were made to stimulate production and in 1650 porcelain paint was sold to Japan. The first porcelain exports from Japan were recorded in 1653. It was not until 1660, though, that exports to Europe rose to any sort of significant level. In 1661 11,500 pieces of Japanese porcelain were imported into the Netherlands. Some of these wares fetched very high prices – understandably, given that there had been nothing at all on the market for almost ten years. There was particularly keen interest in the polychrome painted porcelain. But the Directors of the Company were not really satisfied with the designs and the quality of the painting. 48,000 items were imported in 1663, and about 65,000 in 1665. Supplies to Holland remained erratic and the quantities were small compared with the imports of Chinese porcelain prior to 1645. Between 1669 and 1672, nothing whatsoever was sent to the Netherlands through official channels. Thereafter the quantity was generally below 10,000 pieces a year.

Despite improvements, the quality of the blue painted Japanese porcelain remained inferior to the Chinese. It also cost the Dutch East India Company's buyers much more – roughly twice or three times as much as they had paid for the Chinese porcelain. This meant that a Japanese porcelain plate cost anything from four to nine times as much as a majolica or faience plate or dish made in the Netherlands – too great a difference to be competitive. During the 1660s, and even more in the 1670s, Oriental porcelain for the European market was simply not a worthwhile or very profitable commodity for a company that operated on the scale of the Dutch East India Company. The sea battles in this period, which made overseas imports much more difficult, were an additional complication.

It seems likely that small quantities of porcelain were shipped to Europe by private individuals. In part because it ultimately proved too difficult and too expensive to procure finely made and well-painted blue and white porcelain in Japan, a relatively large number of special orders were undertaken. These were often made according to a wooden model supplied by the customer.

The year 1647 was to be the turning point for the Dutch majolica and faience industry. Koxinga's activities in southern China presented this industry with a new opportunity. The four market leaders, Hendrick van Gogh of De Porceleyne Schotel and Ermpgen of De Porceleyne Lampetkan, both in Delft, and Gerrit Verstraeten and his independently operating father Willem Verstraeten of Haarlem evidently saw the possibilities at once and took appropriate action in 1647, 1648 and 1649. It is clear that these four businessmen had an excellent understanding of the market and were able to respond rapidly to change. Despite primitive means of communication, men like Hendrick van Gogh and Willem Verstraeten were able to take far-reaching policy decisions within a few months.

We have already discussed in the previous chapter the rather unsavoury measures to which Willem Verstraeten resorted in Haarlem at the beginning of 1648 in order to safeguard a share of the new opportunities for himself (pp. 18-21). The manoeuvres that Hendrick van Gogh carried out in Delft in 1647 give a good idea of how tough an operator a businessman could be, and probably had to be, in the 17th century in order to be successful. On 1 May 1647, Van Gogh sold De Porceleyne Schotel to Dirck Jeronimusz van Kessel. Van Kessel had started his career as a young man in De Porceleyne Schotel around 1620. Here he must have learnt all the aspects of the business. In 1640 he set up for himself by purchasing a pottery called De Romeyn, at this time probably still a traditional company producing mainly majolica dishes and tiles. When Van Kessel bought De Porceleyne Schotel, he must have thought that he had acquired a virtually unassailable market position through the combination of his traditional dish and tile company and a faience pottery. De Porceleyne Schotel was not just any company.

'The trade of the porcelain factory, 2 mills, 4 horses, the racks with shelves, a large set of plate moulds, boilers, forms, wheels, tile moulds, 2 copper wash boilers, 2 iron stoves, scrapers (tools used to take off lead and tin oxide), carts, 5 kilns and further all the other equipment, none whatsoever excepted, that in any way belongs to the said porcelain factory and the laundry.' But there was something that Van Kessel had not reckoned with, for on 26 July 1647 Van Gogh bought a building with a plot of land next to a house that he already owned, and immediately started to build a new pottery, Het Gecroond Porceleyn, on this attractive site. The transaction with De Porceleyne Schotel had evidently not been intended as a permanent retirement from business. It clearly did not take Van Kessel long to work out what his former boss's plans were, since on 1 October 1647 he sold De Porceleyne Schotel on to Gysbert Lambertsz Cruyck. With the new owner, the company again found itself with a shrewd operator at the helm – a man who was, moreover, entirely at home in the business. Gysbert's father, Lambert, had been a real entrepreneur who had made a fortune as a flax and cloth merchant and had invested this fortune in all sorts of ventures. One of them was a majolica and tile factory, De Dissel, which he founded in 1640. In the inventory drawn up after his death in 1644, the value of De Dissel and its stock, including 40,000 tiles, accounted for just a small percentage of his immense wealth. His sons Gerrit and Gysbert doubtless became familiar with the business in their father's pottery. Given the future course of Gysbert's life it seems probable that he learnt the potter's trade from top to bottom. In February 1648 Gysbert sold the share in De Dissel that he had inherited to his mother's second husband, Pieter Joppen Oosterlaan, in all probability to give himself more financial capacity for De Porceleyne Schotel. Gysbert ran this pottery for almost a quarter of a century. In 1671 he sold the business to the widow Aelbrecht Keyser, née Vos, who bought the flourishing 'Dutch porcelain factory' with a view to the future of her daughter Anthonia and son-in-law Jacob Pijnacker: Pijnacker bought a quarter of the company from his mother-in-law in 1675, and the rest in 1686.

It seems likely that a rather larger pottery would have been able to produce around 20,000 to 30,000 painted items a year. When imports of Chinese porcelain dried up, it opened up capacity for some ten new potteries, and they rapidly appeared on the scene. Secretive as the owners of the first two firms in Delft – the inventors of the process – may have been about the new techniques in their potteries, when the tide turned in 1647, after more than twenty-five years of production, there was obviously a group of employees and former employees who knew enough about the business to start making the new faience themselves.
By 1665, in consequence, there were already more than twenty faience potteries in Delft, most of which will have produced imitation porcelain *en masse*. There seems to have been no question of over-production. Evidently a proportion of the now old-fashioned majolica, which was still being produced along with tiles in various towns in the Province of Holland, was displaced by the new faience. And there will undoubtedly have been a number of factories that produced faience with minimal decoration, or even unpainted,

for everyday use at the table and in the kitchen. The Delft faience industry was even able to absorb the production capacity of the two Haarlem potteries, which proved not to be viable on the deaths of Willem Verstraeten in 1655 and his son Gerrit in 1657. Delft had thus effectively acquired a monopoly. The concentration after 1650 of a large number of similar businesses in one town had in part to do with the improvement of the product. As long as virtually unprocessed clay was used, independent potteries could exist anywhere. But once they started processing the clay, mixing different types of clay with the aid of water, stirring it and sieving it, which gave a more refined product, clay preparation firms were set up to serve the faience industry. The whole manufacturing process increased in scale. It also made sense to develop these subcontractors to the point where they could supply more than one pottery. Joint glaze mills were founded. These product improvements and scaling up gave the producers of semi-manufactures an opportunity, but this in turn led to a focus on a single type of product or, in other words, specialization.

Faience was produced in Delft possibly together with a few tiles and majolica dishes for use by the peasant class, but these on a very modest scale. Tiles were made in Rotterdam by some twenty tile potteries, predominantly for a rural market. In Harlingen the nucleus of conventional potteries producing majolica and tiles was strong enough for a flourishing tile and flatware industry to grow up there. And Gouda, lastly, was the centre of clay pipe manufacture. Cities like Utrecht

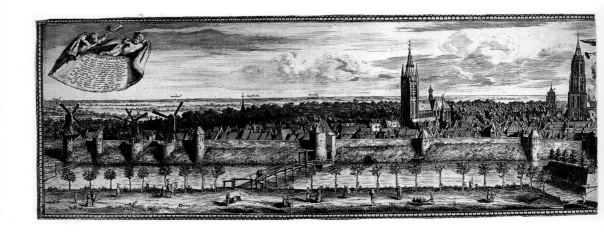

Delft viewed from the west.
The towers of the Oude and
the Nieuwe Kerk are easily
identifiable. Some of the mills
were used to grind the compo-
nents for glaze, a semi-manu-
facture for the potteries.

and Amsterdam retained one or two
tile potteries which succeeded in keeping going until well into the 19th century by specializing in such things as
monumental tile tableaux.

There were several reasons why Delft
succeeded where Haarlem failed. In
1650 Delft had the most viable nucleus
of potteries. There were six firms that
either already made faience or could
very easily switch to this product
because of the knowledge and expertise
they had. This meant that there was a
good basis for expansion. The reason
why a faience industry did not become
established in Haarlem and the whole
sector had actually disappeared by
1700 had to do with the limited number of majolica potters who were able
to change to faience and the fact that
there were only two faience potteries in
the town. When the period of growth
and product improvement dawned, this
was simply not enough. Moreover, the
Verstraetens, father and son, both died
at the very moment that their presence
was crucial. Viewed in this light, it
almost goes without saying that single
businesses in places like Leiden and

Gouda could not survive. And finally,
the circumstances differed from town
to town. Delft had the relative advantage of a location close to clay that was
suitable for the manufacture of faience.
More important still, perhaps, was the
collapse of the once important beer-
brewing industry in Delft. Most of
the breweries had disappeared by 1650.
They had been firms with sizable
commercial premises and relatively
large numbers of workers. Large-scale
faience potteries were easily able to
take their place, and many of them set
up in business in former breweries.
But perhaps it is the human factor
in entrepreneurship that is the most
important factor in the success of a
business. With De Porceleyne Schotel
and later with Het Gecroond Porceleyn, Hendrick van Gogh and Elisabeth Suycker were the pioneers of the
Delft faience industry. To a degree,
their 'pupils' Claes van Straten and
the two brothers Dirck and Pieter van
Kessel did much the same in the 1650s
and 1660s when the industry underwent its dramatic growth. Dirck, for
instance, was one of the founders of

De Paeuw pottery, and he, possibly with his son Steven, laid the foundations for the company known as China. Pieter was the trendsetter at De Vergulde Boot and his son Jeronimus established De 3 Vergulde Astonne. The Van Kessel family was thus responsible for starting four new firms on the basis of the business skills that they had developed in De Romeyn since 1640. The transaction with Hendrick van Gogh and De Porceleyne Schotel and the subsequent sale after a few months was probably viewed in the family as an error of judgment, a minor ripple in a commercial success story. And this gained substance when in the 1650s the opportunities for the faience industry seemed to be almost limitless. Jan, one of Claes van Straten's sons, succeeded his father in De Porceleyne Lampetkan. His daughter Jannetje, married to the cooper Jacob Wemmersz Hoppesteijn, developed into the driving force behind Het Moriaenshooft.

Wealthy outsiders who were willing and able to invest a great deal of money in this capital-intensive industry suddenly started to see unprecedented opportunities. As far as the growth of the industry was concerned, they were arguably even more important than the craftsmen. The two most prominent businessmen to put money into the sector were Wouter van Eenhoorn and Willem Cleffius. Although technically 'outsiders', Van Eenhoorn and Cleffius nonetheless had close ties with the business. Van Eenhoorn married Christijn Lambertdr Cruyck in 1643 and Cleffius married her sister at around the same time. This meant that Van Eenhoorn and Cleffius were brothers-in-law of Gysbert Cruyck,

who acquired De Porceleyne Schotel in 1647. In 1655 Van Eenhoorn made his first investment in the new industry when he bought a half share in De Porceleyne Fles. In 1662, with his brothers-in-law Gysbert Cruyck and Willem Cleffius, he took a quarter share in the acquisition of De Paeuw. In 1663 he sold his share in De Porceleyne Fles, and in 1668 he bought a half share in De 3 Vergulde Astonne. On two occasions the seller was a Van Kessel, who as the first owner had built up a flourishing business from nothing. Van Eenhoorn had other plans for one company. On 17 March 1658 a notarial deed was executed for the purchase of the land and buildings of the former brewery De Griecksche A. In the preceding months, two businessmen had already more or less converted the brewery into a pottery. As a potter himself, Van Eenhoorn built up a flourishing business, regarding the firm as more than a sound investment. On 24 September 1678 Wouter van Eenhoorn gave the successful pottery to his son Samuel, who had been managing it since 1674, as a wedding gift. And there is a similar story about Willem Cleffius. He too made one business, De Metale Pot, over to a son.

In short, a few insiders who were already involved in the trade gave the new industry a tremendous boost. It was financed by a number of entrepreneurs who were sometimes only interested in the money. In a few cases they succeeded in building up one company to such an extent that they laid the foundations for the largest and most successful businesses in Delft. Wouter van Eenhoorn and Willem Cleffius – businessmen with broader horizons –

were probably also able to give the faience industry the stimulus it needed to make 'Dutch porcelain' an international product. They were the people who had the capital needed for businesses on this sort of scale.

There are no known objects from the period up to about 1680 that bear a factory mark or the signature of an owner-potter or of the 'shopkeeper' (the manager of a pottery who had passed the tests required for guild membership) of one of the twenty-five or so companies operating in Delft during this prosperous era. We may conclude from this that there were ample sales opportunities for all the firms; that business was so good for

the potters that a measure to limit free market competition, which is what factory marks essentially are, was not considered sufficiently important for the guild to make it compulsory.

Needless to say, after 350 years, very few of the millions of objects produced by the twenty-five potteries, large and small, in Delft in the thirty years between 1650 and 1680 have survived. Earthenware is breakable, after all, and even if an item did not break during use, the material was so brittle and the glaze so fragile that after a few years a piece was probably so shabby that there was no question of keeping it, let alone cherishing it for a future generation. The simple painted wares that were

11
Dish, c. 1660-1670,
diam. 31.5 cm.

When Chinese porcelain could no longer be obtained, consumers readily bought pieces like this. The Delft dish is the same shape as the Chinese dishes, but it is slightly thicker and consequently rather heavier. The decoration – two birds in a landscape dominated by a bush with a few outsize flowers – is part of the standard repertoire of designs used on the Chinese porcelain of the second quarter of the 17th century.

actually used for eating and drinking have consequently almost entirely vanished. What's more, the few pieces that have survived the ravages of time have not found their way into major museum collections because they are so simple.

The faithful imitations of Chinese porcelain dating from the first half of the 17th century have been better preserved and are more collected. This dish (fig. 11), more than thirty centimetres in diameter, is a fine example of the type. Countless numbers of these carefully painted dishes must have been made for table use and for decorative purposes, for this type is still found in various sizes, with relatively little wear, not only in many museum collections but also in private hands, in quite considerable numbers.

Although Europe was ravaged by wars and unrest before 1650, some of the porcelain imported into the Netherlands must have been exported again – something that happened to a great many of the products that were imported into the country. After about 1660, Germany, slowly recovering from the consequences of the Thirty Years' War, was a keen customer, but now for Delft faience. Alongside fine wares for use, magnificent decorative vases painted with exuberant and delicate chinoiserie were commissioned by many German and Scandinavian royal houses. The finest survivors of this fragile grandeur are in Germany. These objects may have been too large for the Dutch interior, so that the great majority were made for export. The Rijksmuseum has a fine example, however (fig. 12), at present the only one of its kind in a Dutch public collection.

We still have no clear picture of how distribution and exports to other countries were handled. We do know that agents in Amsterdam and The Hague acted as representatives or contacts for foreign customers. In 1668, for instance, the Swedish queen Hedvig Eleonora ordered a crate of earthenware in Delft for 299 silver ducats. Johan van Bommert-Silfvercrona, the Swedish envoy in The Hague since 1650, acted as her agent.

On 1 April 1662, Dirck van Kessel, owner of De Paeuw, received from 'Claude Révérend, merchant of Paris, presently here, 485 guilders for Delft porcelain supplied'. The year before, Révérend had found out all about the pottery business and, according to workers in the potteries, he had come to see for himself how the wares were made, painted and fired. Révérend, it appeared, had much more in mind than simply selling faience made in Delft: with the knowledge he had acquired, he wanted to set up his own 'Dutch porcelain' pottery in Paris. He was not the only person who wanted to establish a Delft pottery outside the Netherlands, but within the sales area of the Delft pottery manufacturers. This was not an easy thing to do, however, without the knowledge of specialists in the business. In the 1660s and 1670s, consequently, several Delft craftsmen were involved in setting up small delftware factories outside the Netherlands. We know that by 1680 delftware potteries had already been set up by Dutchmen or with Dutch craftsmen in Ghent, Hanau, Frankfurt, Paris/St. Cloud, London/Lambeth and Berlin. In the early years, at least, they undoubtedly produced substandard imitations of the Delft products. Technical problems

12
Jar with cover, c. 1660-1670,
h. 62.5 cm.

The jar is decorated with groups of Chinese figures, a flying phoenix and large bunches of flowers, all unrelated and scattered randomly over the curved surface. The decoration is taken from Chinese examples on porcelain dishes, jars and vases. But the totally different arrangement of the 'pictures' and the removal from their context and enlargement of some elements, such as the flowers, means that it bears almost no relationship to the designs on the Chinese objects. This was an entirely individual treatment of unrelated elements to create a new decorative style.

caused by different clays and glazes, limited experience in running such a technically complex business and a relatively small market must have made things difficult for these small firms. The Delft craftsmen who left were doubtless lured by the high wages and perhaps also by the adventure. The fact that the pottery industry in Delft had become an established industry meant that it was very hard for an 'employee' to start a new firm or take over an existing one. Opportunities elsewhere, where the requisite knowledge was lacking, were obviously better. Around 1920 German art historians attributed

much of the faience that had survived in Germany with decoration derived from Chinese porcelain (figs. 11 and 12) to the delftware pottery in Frankfurt. In reality, however, these wares were made in Delft, some as export items for the German royal houses. On arithmetical grounds alone, such an enormous, technically accomplished and varied output would have been impossible in Frankfurt – one firm with a workforce of thirty or so could not possibly have produced more than twenty factories employing some fifteen hundred workers.

Cornelis de Man, *Still life with a Delft jar.* Historisches Museum, Frankfurt.

Cornelis de Man lived and worked in Delft. It is therefore not surprising that he incorporated the latest creations of his fellow-craftsmen, the potters, in his still lifes.

13
Tankard, dated 2 May 1668,
h. 20.4 cm.

The decoration consists of three medallions featuring a violinist, each time in a different setting and with different companions. There is a degree of inconsistency between the drawing-like style of the scenes and figures, and the ornately conceived flower motifs. The pointed lotus petals and the large trumpet blooms of the convolvulus are particularly striking.

Needless to say, with such a huge output, the quality of the design and painting was very varied. Alongside true masterpieces, the potteries also produced a great deal of ordinary painted faience, as well as relatively crude wares that will for the most part have been destined for everyday use. The vast majority of these pieces – and this applies to all qualities – will have been painted with a Chinese or Chinese-style decoration, although the painters also continued to decorate items with finely-painted Dutch landscapes, more or less simple genre scenes, biblical subjects and the very occasional portrait. A relatively high proportion of the small group of objects that were made for special occasions or on commission has survived. These carefully made, usually beautifully decorated occasional pieces are often dated to commemorate some special event. These are objects that were treated with great care and were cherished – not just during the lifetime of their first owners, but also by succeeding generations – and consequently they have been preserved for centuries. The Rijksmuseum has made a point of collecting pieces with a historic or typically 'Dutch' aspect, and the museum's collections have also been enhanced by gifts and bequests over the last hundred years. These models of the Delft potters' art were not usually part of the regular daily factory output; they were, rather, the exception to it. As an illustration of the history of Delft pottery, these pieces thus give a totally misleading impression of what the Delft factories were producing. Over the last century and a half, remarkably enough, this part of the collection of Delft in the Rijks-

museum has increasingly come to govern the image of the Delft earthenware of the second half of the 17th century.

In the Delft faience industry, the focus of product development was the painting. Exceptional pieces were almost always decorated with immense care by the best painter in the factory. Another reason for acquiring a particular piece – aside from a historic or traditionally Dutch background – was often the quality of the painting. The painting is therefore usually the determining factor in the attribution and dating of the fifteen or so exceptional pieces of delftware of the second half of the 17th century shown below.

The shape of this tankard (fig. 13) is derived from versions in stoneware from Westerwald in Germany, which were very popular in the Netherlands in the second half of the 17th century as beer tankards for everyday use. The designers in Delft seldom developed new shapes, instead deriving forms from existing and familiar objects that were used for the same purpose but made of a different material – wood, metal or glass – or from imported ceramics like the German stoneware in this case. No one, it appears, was disconcerted by the fact that the painting on this originally German shape is a combination of bouquets of flowers borrowed from Chinese porcelain and medallions containing Dutch interiors. The piece is dated 2 May 1668. From the preciseness of this date we can infer that this tankard was made on commission, as a gift or a memento of some special occasion. The scenes with the violinist may well have been ordered by the potter especially for this piece from one of the draughtsmen and designers

14
Shoe, c. 1660-1675, h. 8.5 cm,
l. 15.5 cm.

Miniature shoes were evidently popular items which, with a mildly erotic connotation, may well have been intended primarily as an amusing gift. The designs always followed the latest fashions in shoes. Made to measure in leather, this particular model, with its square toe, large bow and substantial heel, would not have been out of place on the foot of a magistrate of this period – a man like Johan de Witt, the Grand Pensionary of Holland.

who worked in Delft during this period. Like tankards, miniature shoes (fig. 14) were made in all sorts and sizes in Delft in the course of two centuries. Here again, flower motifs based on Chinese originals are used on a typically Dutch shape. While the miniature shoes and in this case the tankard, too, can be regarded as gifts ordered for a special occasion, finely painted dishes, individual or in sets, and plates were designed as decorative elements for the houses of more or less well-to-do citizens.

Sets of dishes decorated with a loving couple accompanied by the figure of Cupid, an example of which is shown here (fig. 15), must have been very popular as an element of interior decoration in the 1650s. A set like this would have been displayed at the top of a high wainscot or on the shelf at the end of a great oak bed. There was a high level of standardization in the Delft potteries; without it, it would have been impossible to sustain a production process on this scale. The saggars in which the

pieces were fired varied in size; the largest was about fifty centimetres in diameter, which is why dishes and plates made in Delft are seldom more than forty-eight centimetres across. This large dish is an exception and was consequently not fired in a standard saggar; on the back there are no traces of the pegs on which the dish would have rested had it been fired in the usual way. To protect the dish against flying ash, the workers probably 'built it into' the kiln between saggars with the aid of fire-resistant blocks or other kiln materials.

Among the exceptional pieces dating from the third quarter of the 17th century there are numerous plaques – large flat tiles glazed on both sides. Some of them must have been framed; others have holes in them so that they could be hung up on a cord. In contemporary inventories we find these plaques listed as 'porcelain or china pictures'. Framed, after all, they looked just like small paintings.

Here (fig. 16) the prophet Elijah, who according to the Bible story was fed by ravens by the brook of Cherith, is depicted in a fertile, hilly landscape with three cows. An octagon has been drawn in the glaze on the back of this plaque, as if the painter wanted to see how much of the landscape would still be visible in this format. He evidently liked the effect, as we can see from an octagonal plaque, also dated 1658, which is now in Cambridge, which has a version of the same scene without the prophet Elijah.

The plates, dishes and plaques with portraits or objects relating to the members of the House of Orange, which always provided the stadholder

15
Dish, c. 1650-1665, diam. 53 cm.

The design would lead us to suppose that dishes like this one were probably sold in sets of five. Although in this case there is no legend to support this assumption, the man playing the lute, the woman playing the clavichord and the Cupid holding a songbook symbolize hearing, one of the five senses.

16A
The print by Nicolaas Berchem that the painter used as his example for fig. 16 (see pp. 42-43).

of the most important Dutch provinces, were also special objects. These depictions will not infrequently have had political significance for the person who commissioned them. As stadholder and commander-in-chief of the army until his death in 1647, Frederick Henry, Prince of Orange, promoted his family's interests extremely successfully. He was succeeded by his son William II. In 1650 the 24-year-old stadholder died suddenly, leaving a heavily pregnant wife. Because there was no adult successor to William II, the upper echelons of the citizenry organized in the States of Holland seized the opportunity to curb the Orange influence in government. The period from 1651 to the outbreak of the Third English War in 1672 is known as the First Stadholderless Era. The changes in the political relationships had put the Orangist factions in the Netherlands

16
Plaque, dated 1658, h. 24.5 cm,
w. 30 cm.

For the landscape, the painter
used a print by Nicolaas
Berchem with three Dutch cows
as the main subject. For part of
the decoration, the Delft painter
and draughtsman Leonard
Bramer made a drawing to augment the landscape so that the
whole thing was transformed
more or less into the desired
biblical scene. Bramer provided
a design for Elijah in his own
rapid, sketch-like style. This
plaque was such a complete success in technical terms that the
difference in the drawing styles
between the two fused designs
is still clearly visible in the end
result: Bramer's drawing on the
left and Berchem's print (see
fig. 16A) on the right.

17
Plaque, c. 1655-1665, h. 31 cm,
w. 24 cm.

Unlike most plaques, which
stood in the kiln on either the
long or the short side, propped
up against a small roll of clay,
this plaque was fired flat. One
consequence of this was that the
plaque distorted during firing.

somewhat on the defensive. But on
the other hand, this situation pro-
voked new expressions of loyalty
to the Oranges. Illustrations of the
tomb of the primogenitor of the
Orange dynasty, William the Silent,
for instance, took on great symbolic
value after 1650 (fig. 17).
The front and side aspects of William
the Silent's tomb in Delft's Nieuwe
Kerk, designed by the Amsterdam
sculptor Hendrick de Keyser, were
reproduced several times as a print.
The size of the plaque was dictated

by the dimensions of the engraving by
Cornelis Danckerts which the painter
used as his model for the design. We
may assume that the main outlines of
the engraving were pricked out with a
sharp needle so that the print could be
used as a 'pouncing' stencil. This technique involves transferring a design by
dusting a fine charcoal powder known
as 'pounce' through the perforations in
the stencil, leaving a dotted outline on
the surface beneath. The charcoal powder burns off during the glost firing.

There were also plates and dishes decorated with the portrait of the posthumous son of stadholder William II, who was born in 1650 and also called William (fig. 18). The youthful Prince William III is depicted here on the well of the plate. Although plates with Orange portraits were probably never intended to be used as tableware, it is nevertheless the shape of the standard breakfast plate of the 1630-1670 period. It is rather flat, so that the difference in height between the well and rim is barely perceptible. The double border around the well provided a partial solution to this problem. The pouncing stencil was pricked out from an engraving by Harmanus van Aldewerelt after a painting by the court painter Gerard van Honthorst. The plate remained popular for a very long time. In the late 18th century, when Orange wares were again produced in large quantities (fig. 144), copies of

17A
The tomb of the patriarch of the Orange dynasty, William the Silent, in the Nieuwe Kerk in Delft.

18
Plate, dated 1658, diam. 20.5 cm.

The painter did his job well. The portrait of William III, painted in a strong blue, is flawlessly positioned in the space. The border with festoons of the apples of Orange is perhaps slightly too crowded for a perfect balance between the decoration in the well and on the rim.

19
Inkstand, c. 1670-1680, h. 15 cm, w. 21.5 cm.

The lion's forepaws rest on a shield with the arms of Leiden on the left and Delft on the right. There can be no doubt as to the political affiliations of the owner of this piece: see the *vijva oranie* (long live Orange) on either side of the arms of William III, surrounded by the Garter bearing the motto of the Order of the Garter: *HONI SOIT QUI MAL Y PENSE* (Evil be to him who evil thinks).

20 >
Dish, dated 1675, diam. 39.5 cm.

This dish may have been ordered by the innkeeper, Koenraad 't Hoen, as a lasting memento of the tense war years when the Hollandse Waterlinie or water defence line and the Prince of Orange had played such important roles. The inn was situated just to the east of Woerden, close to the Kamerikker lock, a strategic point in the defence line.

Come will you hurry
to conrad the cockerel
In the kruipin
loyally drink wine there
be merry together
To honour the house of nassau

this 1658 plate were made by De Porceleyne Schotel. On the outbreak of the Third English War in 1672, the Republic was attacked at the same time by land from the south by the huge army of King Louis XIV of France. The Dutch population panicked, William was 'restored' to his position as stadholder and the forces withdrew behind the strategically flooded Hollandse Waterlinie or water defence line. The Orangists among the population now came out more openly in support of their political preferences. Occasionally the arms of the Oranges were painted on an object as a sign of the intended owner's sense of allegiance (fig. 19). The shape of this inkstand is derived from a version in metal, probably pewter. The back of the inkstand is decorated with a painting of a land-scape with a typical Dutch freighter sailing along a waterway. The back is marked *IK*, initials that were attributed in the past to one of the Delft potters of this period. It is more likely, however, that these letters refer not to the maker but to the man or woman for whom the inkstand was intended. In 1675 Jan Knotter of Leiden, a dyed-in-the-wool Orangist, acquired the right to sail to Delft as a barge skipper. The combination of his initials with the arms of towns he linked with his vessel and the decoration on the back would all seem to indicate that he was the first owner of this piece. We do not know for certain that he got the inkstand in 1675, his first year as an accredited bargeman, but the style of the painting and the precise shade of the blue that was used are very similar to those of

the dish dated 1675 (fig. 20) with a picture of a company outside an inn. The inscriptions give us so much to go on, that this object, too, can be rescued from anonymity. The inn called the *Kruipin* is depicted so realistically that the different glasses and tankards can actually be identified. Koenraad

't Hoen, the innkeeper portrayed here, offers the *kertiermeester* (quartermaster) a cool drink. The little dog, referred to by name as Mars, barks at two begging children who are asking for alms with the wonderfully phonetically rendered French phrase: *sy voe plee poveretee* (s'il vous plaît pauvreté). A third man,

47

21
Plaque, dated 1660, h. 18.5 cm,
w. 14 cm.

Robertus Junius, the man
portrayed on this plaque, was
for many years a minister on
the island of Formosa. From
1645 to 1653 he served as a
minister in Delft.

22
Plaque, dated 1662, h. 28 cm,
w. 28 cm.

The plaque depicts the white-
washed interior of a Gothic
church that had been stripped
of all adornment after the
Reformation, when Catholicism
ceased to be the state religion
and Protestantism became the
official faith. A biblical scene
has been set in the church: the
poor widow who casts all she
has, 'two mites, which make a
farthing', into the treasury
(Mark 12). In the 17th century,
biblical scenes like this were
placed in a religious setting
that the viewer could easily
recognize, and the figures
wore contemporary clothes.

Van der Burgh, stands in the inn.
Here again, the coat of arms of Prince
William III is surrounded by the
Garter and the motto accompanied
by the rousing cry, *Vijva Oranie*.

In 1660 a series of portraits of Delft
ministers was reproduced on Delft
plaques (fig. 21). They were taken from
a set of engravings made by Chrispijn
van Queborn in about 1645. It is not
clear why this series of portraits was
put on to delftware in 1660, nor is anything known about the circumstances
in which the portraits were hung. As
early as 1640 a property inventory in

Delft lists 'two octagonal ebony frames
with porcelain paintings'. This plaque
dating from 1662 (fig. 22) must once
have been framed like this. This is the
only explanation for the octagonal
shape and the decoration in the round;
the white corners would have been con-
cealed by the frame.
The little oval plaque with a dune landscape (fig. 23) and the enormous piece
showing an army camp (fig. 24) must
likewise have been mounted in wooden
frames and hung on the wall as paintings. We cannot tell for sure whether
the painter worked from drawings or
with the aid of sketches or engravings

23
Plaque, c. 1650-1665,
diam. 20 cm.

The rugged dune landscape was
painted into the glaze almost
like a pen drawing. The style
is reminiscent of the work of
the Haarlem artist Jacob van
Moscher. The painter in Delft
may have had a single painting
or some drawings by this master
that he could use as examples.

after original paintings. Wild landscapes and army camps were popular
subjects in the third quarter of the
17th century, but they were not among
the specialities of the Delft painters.
The style of painting in the dune landscape is reminiscent of the work of
Jacob van Moscher, and that in the
picture of the army camp on the
plaque of his Haarlem fellow-towns-
man Philips Wouwerman. The fact
that these two pieces are based on
examples or at least sources of inspiration from Haarlem may simply be
a coincidence. But Elisabeth Suycker
and Hendrick van Gogh, owners of
what was arguably the most important
Delft pottery at this time, both came
from Haarlem and they owned a number of paintings by Haarlem masters.
The plaque with the scene of the army
camp, which is more than a metre wide,
must have been fired upright, protected all round against flying ash,
as a special commission. That such
a huge plaque remained more or less
flat and the finely executed painting
did not run can only be described
as a technical miracle.

The number of potteries in Delft shot
up after 1650, and the average size of
these firms must also have grown significantly during this period. In the
larger factories tasks began to be clearly demarcated and divided between
different departments: each individual
had his own job, with one part of the
process being regarded as more prestigious than another. In Delft it was the
painters rather than the modellers who
determined the look of the pieces, and
it may be assumed that the painters as
a group were held in great esteem in
the company. Despite this, we know

very little about their training, whether
they had any opportunity to give their
painting an individual touch within
the constraints of the craft or whether,
for instance, the 'senior painter' drew
the designs and then made a pouncing
stencil for the others to work with. The
vast majority of the pottery painters
in the industry have remained anony-
mous, so that a piece of Delft can at
most be attributed to a particular factory and not to an individual. The Guild
of St Luke, to which all the owners
of potteries and some of the workers
employed in the industry belonged,
had drawn up strict rules aimed first
and foremost at ensuring that the
quality of the product remained high.
The 'masters', for example, had to
produce a proof of their skill and
everyone was obliged to do their work
on the company premises. As a rule,
the painters were forbidden to work
at home. This was probably not just a
question of quality control on the part
of the guild, but also an effort to combat moonlighting. Exceptions were
made to this prohibition, and the
painters concerned, like Frederik van
Frijtom, have sometimes escaped from
anonymity.

24
Plaque, c. 1660-1675, h. 63.5 cm,
w. 101 cm.

Until 1825 this plaque, with its
picture of an army camp, together with another plaque of almost
the same size depicting a mountain landscape, was in the Rijksmuseum voor Schilderijen, the
national gallery of paintings
in the Kloveniersburgwal in
Amsterdam. The items had
found their way, as paintings,
into the Rijksmuseum's collection some time during the first
twenty-five years of the museum's existence, without any
clear provenance or even a date
of acquisition. Upon reflection,
it was decided that they did not
fit in the collection and in 1825
the two pieces, described as
'2 earthenware paintings', were
transferred to the Koninklijk
Kabinet van Zeldzaamheden in
The Hague. The two plaques
were returned to the Rijksmuseum for the opening of
the present building in 1885.

25
Plaque, c. 1670-1695, h. 25.5 cm, w. 33.7 cm.

The painter Frederik van Frijtom took advantage of the white ground in a very individual manner by painting this beautiful Dutch river landscape in various shades of blue with fine outlines and with thousands of minuscule dots. This plaque fits so well into his oeuvre that it can be attributed to him with certainty.

We do not know where or exactly when Van Frijtom was born, but he got married in Delft in 1652 and he will have been about twenty at the time. He was never a member of the guild and probably worked as a freelance for various potteries. At the end of his life he was the 'guild servant' for several years, from which we can conclude that his working at home outside the guild's aegis was accepted by the guild. Van Frijtom signed and sometimes even dated the occasional special piece, which has enabled us to form an idea of his style. A group of plaques (fig. 25),

plates and dishes (fig. 26) can be attributed to him on the grounds of a seldom-used painting technique – which is regarded as his 'signature'. We cannot, however, rule out the possibility that one or more other skilled painters in Delft also worked in his style. When the Rijksmuseum acquired this characteristic dish (fig. 26) in 1962, it had already been on loan to the museum for nearly a hundred years. In 1877 the Belgian owner of the piece, Eugène Albert Garnier-Heldewier, decided that this exceptional dish should be exhibited in the Netherlands. Objects from the second half of the 17th centu-

26
Dish, c. 1670-1685, diam. 39 cm.

The painter Frederik van
Frijtom achieved the unusual
sense of depth in this panoramic
hill landscape by painting the
hills on the horizon in a very
light, almost vanishing blue.

ry with such fine, accomplished painting were already considered as the
best and most desirable pieces that
the Delft industry had produced.
The shape of the plate, which measures
over twenty-five centimetres in diameter (fig. 27), with a flat foot without a
foot-ring, is derived from the group of
small plates of about twenty centimetres across (see figs. 3, 18), which went

out of fashion in the early 1680s. This
shape is not unusual for larger plates
with non-Chinese decoration in the
last quarter of the 17th century. The
well is relatively small compared with
the slightly convex rim.

55

27

Plate, dated 19 September 1685,
diam. 25.5 cm.

The four naked little boys, putti,
in the well hold up a piece of
parchment bearing an edifying
text. A fifth putto hovers above
the scroll with a laurel wreath
and a palm frond, attributes of
victory. The wide rim is decorated with a simple motif of a
crowned and reversed monogram and a text stating that
the plate belonged to a certain
Heleen. The special event on
19 September 1685 for which
this plate was made for the
unknown Heleen is not clear.

If anyone asks be it lad or lass whose
plate I am. Tell them all it is helen
that I recognize

27A

In the 17th century plates
with a flat foot without a foot-
ring and a spreading rim were
typically about 20 to 25 centimetres in diameter.

28
Four plates, c. 1670-1685, diam. 25.5 cm.

The four scenes depict New Testament stories: Christ's entry into Jerusalem, the stoning of St Stephen, the conversion of Saul of Tarsus, and Paul on Malta from the Acts of the Apostles.

The design of these four plates (fig. 28) has been altered slightly in comparison with the example made in 1685 (fig. 27): the well is larger, and the rim stands up slightly. This creates the suggestion of a little painting in a frame. Sets of plates illustrated with scenes from the Bible, like these, were obviously never used as tableware; they were purely for decoration.

A set like this – six or twelve plates with more or less associated biblical scenes – must have been a splendid sight ranged around the top of the oak panelling in the best room of a wealthy family's house. We should not, though, overlook the edifying message of the illustrations, which was part of everyday life for people at this time.

Johannes Vermeer, *View of Delft*. Mauritshuis, The Hague.

Delft viewed from the south. Most of the potteries were in the south and southeast quarters of the city.

Thanks to the technical knowledge built up in the period from 1620 to 1645, the opportunities presented by the cessation of imports of Chinese porcelain and the artistic climate in the Province of Holland, Delft pottery had an immense technical and artistic advantage over everything else being made anywhere in Europe. Delft was undoubtedly at the top of the European earthenware industry very soon after 1650. What Delft was producing was so greatly admired elsewhere in Europe and in the Netherlands that this pottery became the standard at which everyone aimed. This was to remain the case until about 1725. Eventually Delft and delftware were to become a generic name for a single type of product that was made everywhere in Europe, just as the Italian town of Faenza had given its name to the generic name of faience three generations earlier.

The superior Delft products were sold throughout Europe. In many cases, highly placed personages in other countries most probably ordered what they wanted through agents in, for instance, Amsterdam or The Hague. These agents made the contacts and it is debatable as to whether the customer actually knew in which Delft factory his pieces were made. Even despite this relative anonymity, there was apparently no reason to put a 'factory mark' on the products. The ease with which the large number of potteries sold their products will certainly not have given the Guild of St Luke any cause to take steps in that direction. Now, 350 years later, this anonymity is regrettable. The absence of marks means that virtually none of the pieces made in this period can be attributed to a specific pottery. There were various reasons why the potteries in Delft were able to prosper and flourish, but without the sound business acumen of men like Wouter van Eenhoorn and Willem Cleffius, and Jacob Hoppesteijn's wife, Jannetje van Straten, the industry could never have taken off in the way it did. We can see from the story of Jan Aryaensz van Hamme, owner of De Dobbelde Schenckan since 1661, that bad businessmen can get it wrong despite the success of a whole sector. After a few years he stole away from Delft like a thief in the night; he was bankrupt and had succumbed under the burden of his debts. Several months later he turned up in London, beyond the reach of his creditors, and in 1671 he founded a pottery in Lambeth, then just a small village outside London.

Artistic and technical zenith (1680-1720)

The twenty most exciting years (1680-1700)

The Netherlands' political clout in Europe dwindled slowly but surely during the period from 1680 to 1700 until it reached a level appropriate to the size of the country. The French invasion of 1672, during the Third English War, was repelled. The small bishopric of Munster, which had occupied part of the east of the Netherlands in the same year, was forced to sign a peace treaty in 1674 at the same time as a treaty was signed with England. It was not until 1678, after prolonged negotiations, that the Netherlands made peace with France, embodied in the Treaty of Nijmegen.

In 1676 the stadholder William III married the English princess Mary Stuart, daughter of the Duke of York. Some ten years later, as King James II, he attempted to restore Roman Catholicism as the state religion in England, but encountered fierce opposition. The position of the Protestant William III and Mary Stuart became significantly stronger in the European arena when in 1689, after James II had been deposed, they were crowned King and Queen of Great Britain. The English parliament chose to support the Protestant north

against France and the Church of Rome. In 1685 the Edict of Nantes, which had enabled French Protestants to live in relative peace and quiet for almost a hundred years, was revoked. In 1688 France again declared war on the Dutch Republic, a conflict that was to drag on until 1697. With the death of William III in 1702 the political role of the Netherlands, among other things as the guardian of Protestant values in Europe, was essentially over. The childless William III had appointed a nephew as his heir and successor, but the governing class in Holland decided, as they had once before, to leave the post of stadholder unfilled. This period, which was to go down in history as the Second Stadholderless Era, lasted until 1747.

The Netherlands was to remain an important economic power, although its technical and economic advantage over its neighbours was progressively eroded. A broad sector of the population remained prosperous. Trade flourished, with the usual ups and downs, and Amsterdam developed into the financial centre of Europe. The economic situation in the countryside

A selection of new shapes with new decorations was produced to the highest possible standard.

61

varied from region to region and from one period to another. There was a strong upturn during the 1680s so that arable and livestock farming boomed. This was followed by a serious crisis with prices dropping sharply. The farming classes, particularly in North Holland and Friesland, were severely hit by the cattle plague that swept the country after 1720. On the islands of South Holland and Zeeland, where farmers tended to concentrate on growing industrial crops rather than dairy farming, in contrast, the cattle plague had little effect. Unlike farming, industry in the Zaan region enjoyed a period of continuous growth during the first half of the 18th century.

In the third quarter of the 17th century the Dutch East India Company bought limited quantities of Japanese porcelain. The porcelain was intended for the company's own use in Batavia, for trade in Asia and, lastly, for the home market. The official figures entered in the books probably give an incomplete picture. Nevertheless it is clear that imports of porcelain from Japan could only have satisfied a very small part of the demand in the Netherlands for more or less contemporary elegant porcelain for domestic use. In the Japanese town of Arita, the potteries produced both the blue painted wares and porcelain decorated with designs on top of the glaze in brightly coloured enamels. This porcelain – known as *Imari* and *Kakiemon* – was highly sought-after in Europe from the 1660s onwards, and it consequently fetched high prices.

By about 1670 the Manchus had established their authority throughout the whole of China and, after a period of civil disorder and uprisings, peace gradually returned to the country. The manufacture of porcelain in Jingdezhen got into its stride in the 1670s, but it was not until the early 1680s that large quantities of porcelain could again be exported to the Netherlands. This *Kangxi* porcelain, named after the first important emperor of the Manchu Qing dynasty, is delicate and sophisticated, and decorated in a particularly beautiful and strong shade of blue. The finish of these pieces is usually better than that of the export porcelain dating from the first half of the 17th century. During this period, the Chinese, like the Japanese before them, also started to export porcelain that was decorated with overglaze enamels. In the 19th century this coloured Chinese porcelain was classified into different groups by art historians and collectors in France, who gave each group a specific name – *famille verte*, *famille jaune, famille rose* and *famille noire* porcelain. In the 1660s and 1670s, before it was possible to get a wide choice of porcelain from Jingdezhen, the Company must have bought small unpainted objects on a limited scale through Chinese dealers. These pieces came from the porcelain factories of Dehua in Fujian on the South China coast. These unpainted wares, made of a beautifully white translucent porcelain, are now known as *blanc de chine*. The Dutch East India Company also purchased red earthenware teapots from Yixing, likewise in the south of China, probably initially to investigate the commercial possibilities.

In the course of the 17th century there were a great many changes in the houses and the households of the well-to-do citizenry in the Netherlands. Because the water in the densely populated towns and cities in Holland was no longer safe to drink, thirst was generally quenched with a low-alcohol beer known as small beer. In the third quarter of the 17th century, thanks to the overseas trade links, people started to drink tea – at first as well as, and later increasingly instead of beer. The new drinks of coffee and chocolate were also quite common in Dutch towns and cities before 1700. There are earlier reports of the shipment of small parcels of tea via Batavia to the Netherlands, but it was in 1667 that the first large consignment of tea arrived in Amsterdam. Contrary to the expectations of the Dutch East India Company, the tea was very well received by the public. Tea rapidly proved to be a very profitable commodity. Imports on to the Dutch market became regular and increased in volume. New tableware was obviously needed to accommodate the resultant changes in everyday habits. Tea, expensive in the early years, was originally brewed in very small pots, diluted with boiling water and drunk from tiny cups. The small red earthenware teapots from Yixing proved ideal for brewing strong tea.

It was during this period that the young French king Louis XIV built his magnificent Palace of Versailles outside Paris. The design of the palace – both the exterior and the interior – set the tone for court style in Europe. Paintings and statuary, garden layout and objects to decorate the interior always had to be subordinated to the architecture. With the finest craftsmen to be had in France and abroad, a style was developed in Paris that was essentially classical but, through the employment of the most sumptuous materials and the abundant use of ornament, made so opulent that it bordered on the theatrical.

Many thousands of Protestants fled France shortly before and after the revocation of the Edict of Nantes in 1685. Among those who sought a safe haven in the Netherlands was the designer and architect Daniel Marot. He played a major role in the dissemination and rapid acceptance of the new French style in the Netherlands. Within a relatively short space of time after his arrival, the Dutch interior became more crowded and more luxurious. Marot supplied numerous designs to the stadholder, William III, and to the aristocracy in his circle. A great many of his designs were published in the form of prints. One striking aspect is the symmetry in everything that Marot conceived for decorating the home. In consequence, the demand for decorative objects changed. People wanted vases or jars, in pairs or put together into sets, all sorts of small items for étagères and, for the first time, complete dinner services. New shapes were not infrequently derived from examples in silver. For the Delft potteries, as the suppliers of decorative pieces like these, the developments during this period must have been a commercial, technical and artistic challenge.

Growing demand for red earthenware teapots and limited and irregular imports from China meant that prices were high. And, almost inevitably, that some of the potteries in Delft would spend the next few years endeavouring to produce imitations. In the mid 1670s, Ary de Milde who, aside from a brief excursion running his own pottery, had been employed as Wouter van Eenhoorn's master potter since 1658, threw himself into trials with relatively small kilns and experiments with different types of clay. He eventually succeeded in developing a dense, mat reddish brown body, ideal for teapots that were liquid-tight even when unglazed. In 1679 he and Wouter's son, Samuel van Eenhoorn, submitted a patent application to the States of Holland for a process described as 'discovery of the copying and imitation of East Indian teapots, such that the same copied Pots need yield nothing in value and worth to the genuine Indian ones'. If the States was unable to grant the patent, which they requested for a period of fifteen years, they asked that their product might be protected against imitations by a mark. In 1680 they were granted permission to use a mark. Although, technically speaking, these teapots are not regarded as Delft pottery, this story has its place here since this is the first instance of the registration of marks for earthenware in Delft to protect the products, or to combat the competition. After De Milde and Van Eenhoorn had been given permission to use a mark, the States called on all the potteries in the Province of Holland to register their own marks in the event that they wanted to start making teapots of this kind.

The English king, Charles II, had banned imports of delftware at the outbreak of the Third English War in 1672, and the invasion by the French armies must have limited the sales opportunities for the Delft potteries still further. The situation did improve again, but as late as 1684 a delegation was sent from Delft to England to plead for the lifting of the import ban. The image of an uninterrupted boom time for the Delft factories from 1647 to 1724 with just a minor ripple around 1683 because of the resumption of imports of large quantities of Chinese porcelain has to be put into perspective. In the period before and after 1680 there were certainly problems selling to England and France. What finally goaded the guild and the town to abandon its *laissez faire* policy is not entirely clear, but in the early 1680s the potteries started to put marks on many of their wares for the first time. As a rule they used the initials of the owner of the pottery, although the mark was sometimes the name of the company. And so many pieces dating from the last twenty years of the 17th century and the first twenty years of the 18th century can be attributed to a particular pottery. This means that it is also possible to get some idea of the technical and artistic achievements of these firms. During this period, the leading potteries in Delft acquired their own image thanks to the marked products they made.

De Lange Geer in Delft in 2003. In the 17th century this stretch housed four potteries, from left to right: De Grieksche A, De 3 Vergulde Astonne, De Metale Pot and Het Fortuijn.

After the death of his father in 1679, Lambertus Cleffius became sole owner of De Metale Pot. The other children received from the estate De Witte Starre and the share that their father owned in De Paeuw. From the outset De Metale Pot had been a business that was wholly owned and managed. Cleffius Senior had owned De Paeuw together with his brothers-in-law Gysbert Cruyck (entrepreneur in De Porceleyne Schotel) and Wouter van Eenhoorn (entrepreneur in De Grieksche A) and De Witte Starre only with his brother-in-law Cruyck. The three businesses in which Willem Cleffius had an interest were less than a hundred yards apart: De Paeuw diag-

onally opposite De Metale Pot on the south side of the present-day Corn Market and De Witte Starre on the southern spur of the Oude Delft west side. His son Lambertus had worked in the company ever since his father had had the building in De Lange Geer converted into a pottery. We can probably regard him as the hands-on man who actually ran this factory, and his father Willem as a businessman who, with his brothers-in-law Van Eenhoorn and Cruyck, kept a watchful eye on their joint interests. Just as Lambertus Cleffius had worked in his father's business since 1670 and had been given a share in it as a wedding gift upon his marriage in 1672, so it was with his cousin Samuel van Eenhoorn (born 1655), his father Wouter and the former brewery De Grieksche A that Wouter had acquired. Samuel must have worked for his father for a considerable length of time before he received the pottery as a wedding gift in 1678. It may be assumed that his father regarded him as a fully-qualified potter. De Grieksche A was situated in De Lange Geer in the same block as De Metale Pot – they were separated by just one building, De 3 Vergulde Astonne. This had also been a pottery since 1655, and from 1667 it had belonged jointly to Van Eenhoorn and the Kam family. After Wouter van Eenhoorn's death, the heirs disposed of their father's share in the adjacent pottery. It is not impossible that the brothers-in-law bought in supplies jointly for the various factories and passed on to one another large orders that had to be delivered quickly. Be this as it may, the joint interests that these three businessmen had in two companies must have discouraged the three brothers-in-law from tough competition between their 'main works'. We cannot even rule out the possibility that these three men's position in Delft in the third quarter of the 17th century was so dominant that the deaths of Cleffius and Van Eenhoorn in 1679 were among the factors that prompted the guild to take such measures to regulate the market as the registration of marks. In the new business situation, the cousins Samuel van Eenhoorn and Lambertus Cleffius were no longer neighbours, nor did they have any shares in a jointly owned Delft factory, but they must have talked to each other often about the trade and the associat-

ed day-to-day concerns. Despite the contacts and the interaction that must unquestionably have existed between the firms, there is an evident difference between the marked products of De Metale Pot and De Grieksche A. When it is found on objects dating from the second half of the 17th century, the monogram IW is usually attributed to the delftware factory known as Het Moriaenshooft. They are the initials of Jacob Wemmersz Hoppesteijn, who originally owned half and, as of 1664, all of this company. Hoppesteijn was a cooper by trade, and probably never entirely abandoned the occupation. His wife, Jannetje van Straten, was the daughter of Claes Jansz who, after a long period working as a master potter in De Porceleyne Schotel, had been an independent businessman and the owner of De Porceleyne Lampetkan until his death in 1653. His widow, Adriaantje, remarried, and it seems likely that she managed both De Porceleijne Lampetkan and her son-in-law's pottery, Het Moriaenshooft, since ever after 1664, when Jacob had bought out everyone else who had an interest, it was explicitly stipulated that the business was leased to his mother-in-law for another three years. Eventually, her son Jan succeeded her in De Porceleijne Lampetkan and her daughter Jannetje in Het Moriaenshooft. It seems that throughout all these years Jacob Hoppesteijn played only a marginal role in his company.

On Jacob's death in 1671, his widow, with their only son Rochus, became sole owner. That same year, Jannetje remarried. Her second husband was Willem van Teijlingen, the master potter in the factory. After Van Teijlingen's death, Rochus must have been given a more important role in the company. The years when Het Moriaenshooft was run by Jannetje together with her son Rochus are among the most fascinating in the history of the Delft earthenware industry. She died in 1686 and the management of the business passed to her son. Generally speaking we can only deduce how capable the owners of the different delftware factories were in terms of their business acumen and management from how successful their businesses were. Nowadays, we regard the quality of the product as the most important aspect of the business, but in those days the financial results were certainly seen as being more important. A role in the guild may also have conferred status on an owner. The commercial success of a company does not depend solely on the entrepreneur, though; it is also affected by the business climate. During these years, under the management of their various owners, De Metale Pot, De Grieksche A and Het Moriaenshooft produced exceptional and magnificent pieces – the result that matters now. In almost all cases this coincided in these companies with conspicuous commercial success. Without his mother's experience, however, Rochus Hoppesteijn proved to be no businessman. In the space of just a few years he managed to run Het Moriaenshooft into the ground.

The use of five colours in the manufacture of majolica in the early years of the 17th century had in time, after an unmistakable change in taste around 1625, increasingly receded into the background. The only Delft dishes, plates and occasional decorative objects that were painted in more colours than the customary blue were intended for use in rural areas (fig. 10). The interest of the richer sectors of the population in Europe in the polychrome Japanese Arita porcelain painted with enamels may well have set the leading delftware manufacturers thinking in the 1670s. In addition to bright colours like yellow, green and blue, the Japanese painters initially used a dark aubergine and a lot of rather dull dark red. In most types of porcelain, blue was the only colour that was painted directly on to the porcelain before the second firing.

In Delft the potters were accustomed to letting the whole of the painted decoration fuse with the white glaze during the second or 'glost' firing. The consequence of this method was that the only pigments that could be used in the delftware industry were those that could withstand a temperature of around 950 degrees Celsius in the kiln. The glaze has to reach this temperature during firing before it will melt completely to form a vitreous layer. The colours that can be used are based on metal oxides; any colours made from organic pigments burn at that temperature. And the colours gold and red could not withstand this high firing temperature either.

However, the Delft faience painter Jeremias Godtling appears to have mastered the technique of firing the

29

Dish, c. 1680-1685, attributed to Het Moriaenshooft under the management of Jannetje van Straten, diam. 38.5 cm.

The family coat of arms on this dish was borne by four Dukes of Brunswick and Lüneburg in the second half of the 17th century. It is possible that this could be a gift dating from 1682, when Sophia of Brunswick married her cousin George, the oldest son of Duke Ernst August and the Dutch-born Sophia, daughter of Frederick of the Palatinate. Through his mother's descent, George was to succeed to the throne of Great Britain in 1714.

30 (pp. 70-71)

Two dishes, c. 1685-1690, attributed to Het Moriaenshooft under the management of Rochus Hoppesteijn, w. 33 cm, d. 26 cm.

During this period, sets of small trays or dishes were designed so that they could be arranged around a central piece to form a star. 'Preserve sets' like this were placed in the centre of the table and filled with all sorts of sweet or savoury delicacies.

colours effectively on top of the glaze at a temperature of about 600 degrees Celsius. It seems likely that he learned this specialism in Amsterdam, where we know he spent at least a year, probably in a studio making stained glass, or he may even have learned to enamel on a copper surface. Be this as it may, in 1679 a new era dawned for Jannetje van Straten in Het Moriaenshooft. Her second husband, the potter Willem van Teijlingen, died in that year and her son Rochus was still too young to run the company on his own. Jannetje may have hired the experienced Jeremias Godtling at this time. About 1680 Het Moriaenshooft started to produce dishes and vases painted in colour with Italian and mythological scenes in blue, surrounded by cupids and ornaments in blue, green and purple, conventionally painted in the glaze, heightened here and there with the colours red and gold, which were fixed in a third firing at a lower temperature (fig. 29). This group, which is usually marked with the initials IW, is attributed to Het Moriaenshooft in the years that Jannetje van Straten managed the factory (1679-1686). She must have relied on Godtling's knowledge and skill for the technical execution of the colours red and gold, which were new to Delft at this time. These sophisticated, colourful wares became a *nouveauté*, intended for the highest classes in Europe, given the subject of the decoration, here the castration of Uranus by Chronos, and the sumptuous execution using colour.

After Jannetje's death, control of the company passed into the hands of her son Rochus. He must have had a very good feel for what the trend-setting elite wanted in terms of show – generously proportioned decorative pieces, covered with a beautifully white glaze, and painted with a refined decoration that was executed with an eye for detail. Commercially, however, the business rapidly went downhill very soon after the death of his mother. Evidently he was not able to make money from these magnificent pieces. In 1688 Jeremias Godtling left to set up his own pottery with others in The Hague. Rochus probably took on Gijsbrecht Verhaest as his new man, however a document relating to legal proceedings reveals that he had little authority over him. In 1690 the business was split into two – evidently there were at least two main kilns – and Rochus sold one part, which was continued under the name Het Oude Moriaenshooft. He kept the other part himself, running it under the name Het Jonge Moriaenshooft. It is probable that no more special pieces decorated in polychrome were made after this split in 1690. If he needed such items, he ordered them from Jeremias Godtling in The Hague. Rochus died on 25 March 1692, and his estate proved to be insolvent. Rochus's widow refused to accept the legacy. In July the business was bought by Lieve van Dalen.

The two dishes (fig. 30) were originally part of a composite set that consisted of another two dishes the same shape, between which two smaller and two larger trapezium shaped dishes could be placed. In the centre there would have been a elongated octagonal dish. In the literature pieces like this are described as 'rijsttafel sets', a description that accords with the use to which people would put sets of dishes like this nowadays, but cannot possibly be

31
Teapot, c. 1685-1690, attributed to Het Moriaenshooft under the management of Rochus Hoppesteijn, h. 17.2 cm.

The shape of the pot is derived from an example in Chinese porcelain, probably the undecorated *blanc de chine*. In China pots like this were used for hot wine.

31A
The manufacturer of the little pot, Rochus Hoppesteijn, evidently found the result so special in terms of shape and decoration that he marked it not only with his initials RHS but also with the head of a Moor, the illustration of the name of his pottery, Het Moriaenshooft.

correct because people in Western Europe were unfamiliar with Indonesian food in the 17th century. In old inventories there are references to 'preserve sets'. It is much more likely, therefore, that we should visualize these as a sort of table centrepiece containing all sorts of sweet or savoury relishes and preserves to be eaten as accompaniments to the main course or the dessert. The huge dinner service that was ordered from Lambertus Cleffius in about 1685 (p. 81) originally had at least six sets like this, all of them comprising rather smaller dishes. The complete service must have made an overwhelming impression on the guests at the table. Plaster moulds must have been made for the little teapot (fig. 31). It is not possible to throw a piece with so many angles.

Even before Jannetje van Straten started experimenting with colour in Het Moriaenshooft around 1680, there had already been a cautious move away

from blue as the only colour in Delft. After half a century, monochrome decoration must have become a tradition for Delft painters that was essentially unchallengeable. No one in the industry had ever painted the best pieces in anything but blue. Sometimes, to suggest perspective, the colour blue was applied in different shades. Painters did use a darker shade for outlines; it was achieved by adding rust to the blue, which turned it almost black. It consequently bears witness to great daring to suddenly paint important decorative pieces in two colours, blue and purple. This colour combination, possibly inspired by Japanese and Chinese porcelain that was decorated in more than one colour, is typical of the 1670s. The earliest pieces in two colours were made before the introduction of factory marks on delftware, so that we can do no more than make an educated guess as to the potteries that first took this bold step. It seems most likely to have been one of the businesses that were to come to the fore with such flair

32
Jar with cover, c. 1670-1685,
h. 83.5 cm.

The scenes, which are not large,
are placed separately and without much connection on the
surface. The size, the decoration
and the addition of purple made
this jar an impressive piece.

and sense of new opportunities after
1680: De Metale Pot, De Grieksche A
or Het Moriaenshooft. For the model
of the large pot with a lid (fig. 32) the
factory had to come up with a technical
solution to the problem of making a
round shape octagonal. The potter
used so much clay for the wall of the
pot when he threw it that there was
enough thickness to cut and shave
pieces off vertically from the round
pot to create eight equal planes. As
decoration the foot and the neck were

finished with a row of large palmettes,
between which the space, in contrast
to the large pieces dating from the
1660s, is left open. The small scenes
that are scattered without connection
across the surface, are however essentially unchanged in comparison with
the pot made a few years before (p. 36,
fig. 12). The pot is so large that one
can only imagine a piece like this in
a grand salon.
The vase (fig. 33) is decorated with
landscapes on three levels. Here again,

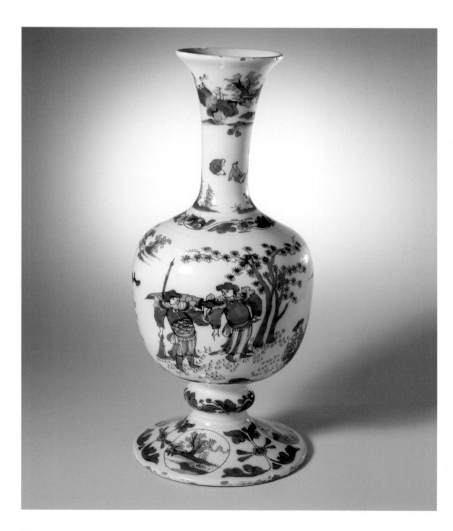

33
Vase, c. 1670-1685, h. 30 cm.

The vase is one of a group of
objects in the Rijksmuseum,
which are painted in a rather
greyish light blue in combination with a soft purple and
which generally have rather
sparse decoration.

34

Dish, c. 1680-1685, attributed
to De Grieksche A under the
management of Samuel van
Eenhoorn, diam. 48.5 cm.

The painter has seized the
opportunity to make the figures
more expressive by playing with
the colour purple in the figures'
clothes and in the brushstrokes
with which the faces are built up.

there are no continuous scenes, simply
separate decorations placed above and
next to one another. The design and
the refinement of the painting mean
that this object is a vase that would
never have been used as such, but was
a decorative element in the furnishing
of a house.

The dish (fig. 34) and the spice jar
with a cover (fig. 35) are both marked
with the initials of Samuel van Eenhoorn (SVE), who succeeded his

father Wouter as owner of De Grieksche A in 1678. In terms of shape and
decoration, the dish is still true to the
tradition of the 1660s and 1670s; only
the use of purple is new. The painter
has seized the opportunity to make the
figures more expressive by playing with
colour in the clothes and in the brushstrokes with which the faces are built
up. The whole thing is an impressive
decorative piece almost fifty centimetres in diameter, the largest size that

could be produced. In designing the shape of the spice jar the modeller probably looked at an object designed for the same purpose, but made of silver. Around 1680 the shape was still so new in earthenware that the painter had difficulty achieving a balanced decoration for the pot and the lid. He painted alternate sections with a tiny landscape with Chinese figures and a flower design. Below the monogram SVE is the number 24, a code for identification in the factory or by the customer.

During this period the potteries were able to supply a wide range of items.

Almost every factory produced pieces painted with their own interpretations of the decorations on the Chinese porcelain of the 1670s and 1680s, as well as objects that were decorated with all sorts of European subjects. A great many beautifully decorated high-quality items for use and ornamental pieces were produced. The impression is that the proportion of occasional pieces was a small minority of these. Most of the objects of this period have a factory mark. The pieces decorated in the Chinese manner are similar in terms of style to the items painted in blue and purple (figs. 32-35).

36
Dish, c. 1680-1690, attributed
to De Metale Pot under the
management of Lambertus
Cleffius, diam. 30.5 cm.

The area in which Chinese
figures stand is indicated with
a simple setting of a fence,
spinneys and a length of painted
silk. The scene was not placed
centrally on the surface; there
is open space on the left giving
the decoration an even more
Oriental feel. The border, which
has been left relatively 'empty',
is painted with a fairly simple
design of flowering branches.

37
Ornament, c. 1680-1690,
attributed to De Metale Pot
under the management of
Lambertus Cleffius, h. 25 cm.

Two Chinese figures beside a
small table have been painted on
one side of this octagonal flattened sphere. Their surround-
ings have been left empty. The
other side, in contrast, is filled
with two standing and two
seated Chinese, one of whom
belligerently holds a scimitar
aloft. The top is ringed with
palmettes. The painter evidently found it hard to devise
a suitable decoration, balanced
on all sides, for such a new
object.

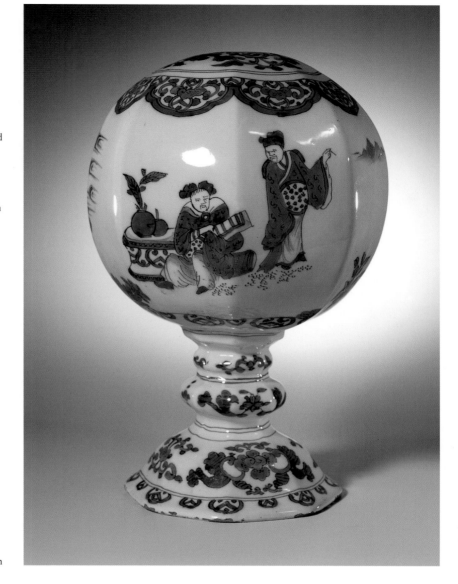

Open, fairly sparse decoration is characteristic of the style of De Metale Pot
in the 1680s (fig. 36). The painter who
made the designs for the dishes and
plates departed from the general tendency in Delft to cram the object as
full of decoration as was humanly
possible. Possibly influenced by
the decorations on Japanese porcelain,
he was brave enough to leave empty
space.

This object (fig. 37) is sometimes
described in the romanticizing literature as a wig stand. However since
both small (too small) and extremely
large versions of this shape exist, it is

38

Teapot, c. 1680-1690, attributed to De Metale Pot under the management of Lambertus Cleffius, h. 11.5 cm.

Teapots this shape are still being produced today. This shows just how important the interaction between the Orient and Delft at this time was in the development of the design of everyday objects.

39

Small dish, c. 1680-1690, attributed to De Grieksche A under the management of Samuel van Eenhoorn, diam. 13.9 cm.

This shape, a peach leaf, was very popular in Japan. This Delft version is a free interpretation of it.

much more likely to be an object that was originally one of a pair gracing a table or possibly a shelf in the panelling of a room.

It can be seen from the shape of the little teapot (fig. 38) how important this period in Delft was for the design of everyday objects in Europe. Now, more than three centuries later, teapots in this shape are still being produced. The decoration is of its time or, one might say, 'dated', and the use of different materials means that modern teapots are rather more streamlined, but in essence not much has changed in three centuries.

Probably influenced by the dinner services that were designed in silver for Louis XIV, the European elite gradually felt a need to lay their dining tables with sets of plates, dishes, platters and bowls of varying sizes which matched in shape and decoration. Other objects that were used on and around the dining table, items like salt cellars, cruets for oil and vinegar, spice and sugar castors, candlesticks, water jugs and wine coolers, could be harmonized

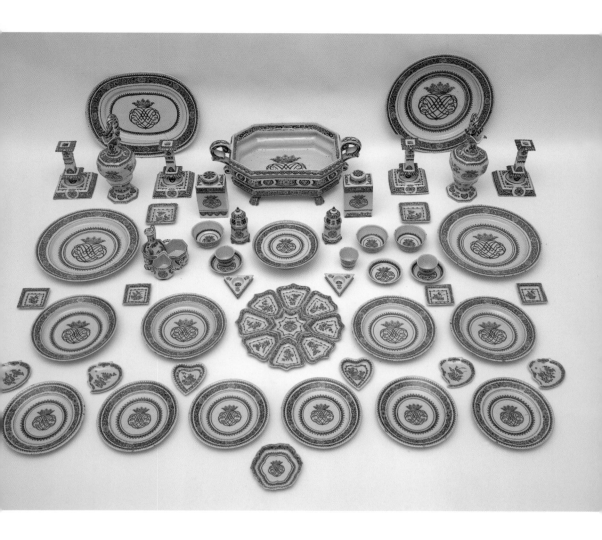

Many pieces of this large dinner service, supplied by Lambertus Cleffius around 1685, have remained together.

in shape and, above all, in decoration when they were made of tin-glazed earthenware. Services like these were completely new and the designers must have looked around them very carefully to see which shapes could be put together. For most pieces they must have looked at contemporary objects in silver, although this does raise the question as to where a potter in Delft around 1680 could have seen a full

service in silver in his home town. Or did he perhaps do more creative work than we give him credit for today? In the 1680s Lambertus Cleffius supplied a large dinner service, decorated with a double monogram for the client who commissioned it, Wenzel Ferdinand, Prince Lobkowicz (see above). The Rijksmuseum has several pieces from similar services made by De Grieksche A during the same period

40

Candlestick, c. 1680-1690, attributed to De Grieksche A under the management of Samuel van Eenhoorn, h. 25.5 cm, diam. foot 19 cm.

The pseudo-Chinese characters decorating the shaft of the candlestick are particularly striking. The shape is borrowed from a model in Dutch silver, popular at this time.

– a small dish (fig. 39), a candlestick (fig. 40) and a salt cellar (fig. 41). The dish is marked SVE 18, the candlestick SVE 10 and the salt cellar SVE 3. This was an efficient way of indicating the model and size. The little dish is in the shape of a peach leaf, a shape that was very popular in Japan and was produced in China on a large scale for the Japanese market in the 17th century. The style of the rim decoration is reminiscent of that of De Metale Pot, but the space is filled more completely, and the little landscape, similar as it is, has a less robust feel to it thanks to the subtle structuring of water, landscape

and background. The candlestick and salt cellar were both designed after examples in silver and the painter has subordinated the decoration to the shape. Each lobe of the salt cellar has a tiny individual landscape. The six lobes of the foot of the candlestick alternate between a landscape with Chinese figures and a stylized tulip, a motif derived from the Chinese porcelain dishes of the 1640s. The pseudo-Chinese characters decorating the salt cellar and the shaft of the candlestick are particularly striking. In De Grieksche A's studio, to an extent borrowing from existing designs, the

41

Salt cellar, c. 1680-1690, attributed to De Grieksche A under the management of Samuel van Eenhoorn, h. 10.8 cm, diam. 12 cm.

Contrary to the Delft custom, the painter has subordinated the decoration to the shape. The salt originally sat like a little mountain in the cavity.

42

Flask, c. 1680-1690, attributed to De Grieksche A under the management of Samuel van Eenhoorn, h. 42 cm.

A silver flask almost certainly served as the model for this piece. The leaves above the foot were not painted but are made in relief, something that was unusual in Delft.

painters were creating something new on what were then modern shapes. The flask (fig. 42) may also have been used at the table and likewise been part of a service. The flattened round shape has been borrowed from an originally mid 16th-century Italian idea. Countless examples of majolica from Urbino, beautifully painted with mythological scenes, have survived. It is unlikely that Samuel van Eenhoorn would have been familiar with these Italian 'field flasks'. The example he had in mind for this flask, or the one that was shown to him by the first person to commission one, was most probably a flask made of silver. The designer in the factory took the leaves above the foot, so typical of the elaborate, often relief, decoration of the silver of this period, and reproduced them not by painting them but in relief, something that was highly unusual in 17th-century Delft earthenware. The designers were not afraid to tackle difficult shapes, but they nonetheless thought first and foremost of a painted decoration, which was usually considered more important than the shape. The satyr heads acquired the face of a 17th-century cherub and the designer simply omitted the rings that were always present above the mask. Existing pouncing stencils were used for the beautifully executed decoration. From the remaining pieces of the dinner service that survive in Nelahozeves Castle in the Czech Republic (p. 81), it can be seen that each object was supplied at least as a pair, but usually as a multiple of pairs. The candlestick and the salt cellar, and probably the flask too, are the survivors of huge services which originally consisted of sets of identical pieces.

Samuel van Eenhoorn died in 1685. His widow Cecilia Houwaert ran the pottery for a year after his death. In 1686 she sold it to her brother-in-law Adrianus Kocks, a merchant in Rotterdam, who registered with the guild as a 'shopkeeper' in 1687. Adrianus Kocks and his wife Judith van Eenhoorn took the pottery that came from the estate of Judith's deceased brother Samuel, De Grieksche A, to even greater heights. This was the factory that supplied the faience to the English court, ruled by the Dutch William III and his wife Mary Stuart since 1689. Ensembles of large vases, flower holders and bases for jugs of a size that was in keeping with the huge ceremonial rooms in the new palace of Hampton Court were made in De Grieksche A. The aristocracy who moved in the circle of the king and the queen also ordered delftware of a sophistication and elegance unprecedented in the Netherlands. Since about 1940 the monogram AK on objects dating from this period has been linked with reasonable certainty to De Grieksche A in the years that Kocks was the owner.

Large rectangular caddies with covers (fig. 43) were part of the regular repertoire of objects that went to make up a dinner service at this time. It is possible that they were meant for tea, but in view of how expensive tea still was, they really seem too large for this purpose. The screw thread on the neck and inside the cover was a new feature at this time, and one that considerably enhanced the usefulness of the object. With its superb, delicate execution, the little dish (fig. 44), which is only sixteen centimetres in diameter, speaks for itself.

43

Caddy with screw cover,
c. 1685-1695, attributed to
De Grieksche A under the
management of Adrianus Kocks,
h. 27.3 cm, w. 13 cm, d. 9 cm.

This caddy was once part of
a large service that may have
graced the table of the Austrian
Counts of Zinzendorf. Items
from this service can be found
in many European museums
and private collections.

Costly as these pieces were, inevitably in every household objects were sometimes broken during use. In the absence of good glues that were suitable for earthenware and porcelain, 'riveting' was the only way to put a broken piece back together again.

By drilling small holes opposite one another on either side of the break and connecting them with tiny metal strips known as rivets, it was possible to keep the pieces together, but the object could no longer be used. If there was just a chip out of the rim,

the edge could be ground down all round or even ground away altogether. The bottom of a dish treated like this could then be given a second lease of life by putting a border of wicker or wood around it. The maker of the Delft basket (fig. 45) probably took as his example a basket with a porcelain bottom and sides made from wicker-work or carved out of limewood. The suppleness of the material that served as the model can be seen in the scrolls, the border and the handles.

44

Dish, c. 1685-1695, attributed to De Grieksche A under the management of Adrianus Kocks, diam. 16 cm.

With its refined decoration and superb execution, this piece comes close to the excellence of the Chinese porcelain of the period.

45

Basket, c. 1680-1690, h. 6.5 cm, diam. 34.5 cm.

The base is decorated with some Chinese figures holding a parasol, a pack on a stick and other baggage. The open space has been filled in three places, among other things with a small landscape and two scroll paint-ings. Unusually for delftware, the wall of the basket has been left undecorated.

46
Water container for birds,
c. 1680-1685, attributed to
Het Moriaenshooft under the
management of Jannetje van
Straten, h. 17.5 cm.

The painter of this object, which
was probably quite unfamiliar
to him, used elements of
larger decorations to achieve
a balanced design.

47 (pp. 90-91)
Pair of ornamental vases,
c. 1685-1690, attributed to
Het Moriaenshooft under the
management of Rochus
Hoppesteijn, h. 46 cm.

The subject of the decoration
may well refer to the use to
which the pieces would be put –
as ornaments on the balustrade
in a formal garden.

48 (pp. 92-93)
Pair of plaques, c. 1690-1705,
attributed to De Witte Starre
under the management of
Dirck Witsenburgh or Dammas
Hoffdijck, h. 39 cm, w. 37.5 cm.

The borders of these plaques,
moulded into the plaques
themselves, imitate a carved
wooden frame. Frames as
ornate as this must have been
exceptional, even in wood.

Although the painted decoration on
this object (fig. 46) is exceptionally
fine, it was nonetheless probably conceived of as a piece that would have
been in regular everyday use as a
drinking vessel for birds in an aviary
or in a large cage in the house.
The model of these decorative vases
(fig. 47) like the 'field flask' (fig. 42)
is derived from an older example from
Italy. The handles are formed in part
from a lion's head with a ring and
dangling mane. A vase of the same
shape which, on the grounds of the
monogram IW, used in Het Moriaenshooft in Jannetje van Straten's time,
can be dated before 1686, is decorated
with landscapes with peacocks derived
from Chinese porcelain. Another
example, which is also marked IW,
has as its subject two stories from
Ovid's *Metamorphoses*.
The pair in the Rijksmuseum, which
is not marked, has a painting of two
women sitting in a garden on one side,
and a woman with a horn of plenty
being supported by angels on the other.
The angels are similar to the putti on
the plate dated 1685 that was discussed
in the previous chapter (p. 56, fig. 27).
In the light of the unanimity of form
of all the vases, those in the Rijksmuseum can also be attributed to
Het Moriaenshooft. The quality
of this group of vases testifies to the
high standard that the factory run by
Jannetje van Straten and her son in
the 1680s had achieved. It is clear that
the leading Delft potteries already
had a good sense of the prevailing
European fashion when the French
architect Daniel Marot arrived in the
Netherlands.

De Witte Starre, one of the potteries
in Willem Cleffius's estate, went its
own way under the management of
its master potter Dirck Witsenburgh.
Although it was owned by one of
Cleffius's sons, Henricus, until about
1705, he has to be regarded as a sleep-
ing partner who was the owner in ever
changing shares – first half, then the
whole thing, then three-quarters.
After 1705 the company was owned
for a while by the potters Dammas
Hoffdijck and Jacobus de Lange, who
also owned De Roos, and in consequence the decoration of the objects
from the two factories increasingly
came to resemble each other. The two
plaques (fig. 48) are decorated with
panoramic landscapes peopled with
figures wearing typical Dutch dress.
Plaques were initially no more than
slightly thicker, larger tiles. They
could not be hung on a wall without
a support – in the 17th century this
would have been a wooden frame. In
the 19th and 20th centuries people
considered 17th-century plaques as
objects that belonged in a collection
of delftware, possibly even as the most
important examples of the early period
of Delft manufacture. As a result, they
were displayed in glass cases along
with dishes and other Delft objects.
Wooden frames, particularly around
the smaller plaques, no longer ac-
corded with the views of these collectors, and so they were removed. With
the emphasis on refinement in the
Delft industry during the last decades
of the 17th century, the designers in
some of the factories came up with
the idea of manufacturing plaques
with moulded borders, forming a
whole with the flat plaque. From the
pair of plaques by De Witte Starre we

49
Ornamental flask, c. 1700-1710, attributed to De Witte Starre under the management of Dirck Witsenburgh or Dammas Hoffdijck, h. 28.5 cm.

Under a circlet of angel heads and a neck decorated with clouds in which angels hover, the eight facets of the flask-shaped vase depict Christ wearing the crown of thorns, Peter, Matthew, Luke, John the Baptist, Bartholomew, Thomas and the Virgin as half-length figures with their attributes.

50 >
Pair of flower holders, c. 1690-1700, attributed to De Grieksche A under the management of Adrianus Kocks, h. 11 cm, w. 26 cm, d. 8 cm.

Each of the four facets of the rectangular flower holders is painted with a different land-scape, although they are related in style. The top has round holes through which the water can be poured and in which the flowers can be arranged. These are superb objects whose flat sides provided the opportunity to vary the decoration. This new design finally came into fashion in England a quarter of a century later; so far these are the only known examples from Delft.

can get an idea of how the other plaques must originally have looked with their frames. The borders of this pair imitate a carved wooden frame with medallions containing putti, flowers and, in the corners, an outward-facing leaf. The eye is drawn to the top of the frame by two alligators. Frames that were as ornate as this must, however, have been the exception.

This outstanding ornamental flask comes from the same pottery (fig. 49). In view of the figures depicted on it, a vase like this can only be envisioned in a Catholic setting – in a home, or possibly as an ornament on an altar. In liberal Holland, Catholics were able to worship both in church and in private. There are at least two other surviving versions of this vase, more or less identical, one with the De Roos mark and one without a mark.

Just how confusing the attribution of objects to a particular factory solely on the grounds of a mark can be, even for an expert, can be seen from these marked flower holders (fig. 50). On the grounds of the painting on the two

51
Violin, c. 1705-1710, h. 63 cm, w. 22 cm.

The virtuosity with which the front, a long, narrow area, has been filled with a ballroom with high windows and a sort of balcony on which a small orchestra plays, testifies to the mastery of the painter (see p. 6). The back is decorated with a scene in front of an inn: a violinist on a dais around which a cheerful company dances. The space is cleverly filled with the two storey-high façade of the inn.

plaques and the flask (figs. 48 and 49) an attribution to the same pottery or to De Roos would seem to be obvious. However, the monogram AK, with which the flower holder is marked, is associated with Adrianus Kocks, the third owner of De Grieksche A. The style of the decoration is more likely to have come from one prominent painter who was working for the factory at the time. Here, the most probable candidate is the delftware painter Jeremias Godtling, whom we have already met. He seems to have started his career at De Roos shortly after 1660, considered moving to Paris in 1667, and spent at least a year with his wife and children

living and working in Amsterdam between 1676 and 1678. After that he worked for Jannetje van Straten in Het Moriaenshooft and in 1689 he was a partner in his own pottery in The Hague. In January 1693 he went to work for Kocks in De Grieksche A. Godtling took his characteristic manner from employer to employer throughout his career, while he must have left some of the tools of the trade, such as the pouncing stencils, behind him here and there. At the same time, younger painters in the various potteries must have adopted his painting style. It is consequently perfectly possible for objects painted in the same

An etching of the most important piece in the Van Romondt
collection in Utrecht was made
by Leopold Flameng in 1876
specially for the catalogue of
the collection.

style to have come from different
factories, and it is possible that they
could have been created long after the
person who conceived them had left
or even died.

On 11 to 13 July 1876, in the Arts and
Sciences Building in Utrecht, the
Amsterdam auctioneers C.F. Roos
and Son auctioned the art collection
belonging to Wilhelmus G.F. van
Romondt. The chapter on 'céramique'
in the catalogue, which was written
in French by Henri Havard, starts
with 'lot no. 383: Violon en faience de
Delft' (fig. 51). This object, to which

Havard devoted one-and-a-half pages
of minute and rapturous description,
was regarded at the time as the most
important piece of Delft faience in the
world. The purchaser was the collector
John F. Loudon, who by acquiring
this piece was able to more or less
complete his collection. Although the
assessment of this piece is perhaps not
quite so clear-cut after a hundred and
twenty-five years, this violin is always
included and illustrated in any publication about delftware. This exceptional
object was neither marked nor signed.
In feeling and style, it resembles the
two plaques, the ornamental flask
and the two flower holders discussed
above.

The faience industry in Delft was so
focused on decorating the objects with
superb painting that the design did not
always get the attention it deserved. The
trade's long history and the immense
experience of the people working in it
meant that there was usually no problem whatsoever with dishes, vases and
jars thrown on a wheel, but when more
complicated shapes had to be made
the lack of a designer was sometimes
painfully obvious. When Lambertus
van Eenhoorn, Wouter's second son,
bought De Metale Pot from the estate
of his recently deceased cousin Lambertus Cleffius in 1691, he must have
been aware of this gap in the business.
On 25 July 1691 Van Eenhoorn hired a
Frenchman called Guillaume Nieullet
as a modeller. In 1693 his contract was
renewed for ten years. It was explicitly
stated in this document that in the
event of Nieullet's death all the moulds
used by him would become Van Eenhoorn's property. In some deeds he is
referred to as a 'carver'.

52
Bust of Prince William III of
Orange as King of Great Britain,
attributed to De Metale Pot
under the management of
Lambertus van Eenhoorn,
c. 1695-1700, h. 42 cm.

In this portrait, which derives
its expression and likeness to
the king from the modelling,
the decoration has been totally
subordinated to the form.
De Metale Pot hired a 'sculptor',
the Frenchman Guillaume
Nieullet, specifically to make
the models.

The presence of a modeller employed
specifically to produce complex designs
is clear from the output of the factory
during his time there. The portrait
bust of William III as King of England
(fig. 52) in this form could not conceiv-
ably have been made anywhere but in

De Metale Pot during this period.
It is first and foremost the modelling
that makes it a successful portrait. The
obelisk (fig. 53) is also well designed.
This tall object, probably one of a pair,
must originally have stood with its
mate as an ornament on a table or

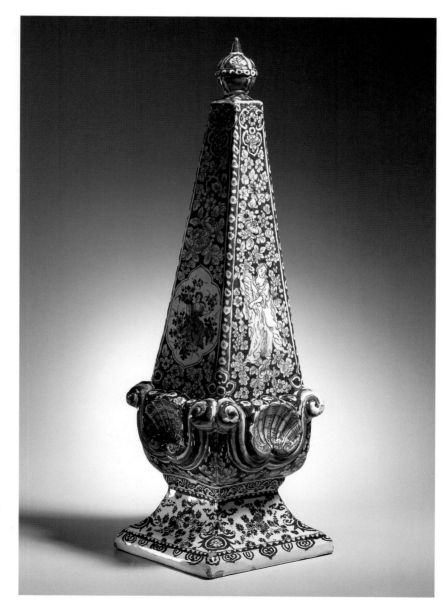

53
Obelisk, c. 1695-1710, attributed
to De Metale Pot under the
management of Lambertus van
Eenhoorn, h. 48.5 cm.

A faience obelisk like this reveals
how the potteries in Delft drew
their ideas for shapes from all
sorts of sources, adapted them
to a new use, and then conceived
an appropriate decoration for
them.

54

Pair of flower holders in the shape of a stacked obelisk, c. 1710-1720, attributed to De Metale Pot under the management of Lambertus van Eenhoorn, h. 104 cm.

In spring, flower holders like this could be filled with tulips, so beloved and so expensive at this time, but they look magnificent with other flowers too. The panels on the base are decorated alternately with a female figure carrying a cornucopia as 'Flora' and two peacocks in a landscape.

sideboard, or perhaps as a permanent feature on a mantelpiece. The pair of tall flower holders (fig. 54) has several design elements in common with the obelisk, at least more than with a pyramid after which pyramid flower or tulip vases are called in the jargon of collectors and antique dealers. The piece is made up of nine tiers on a base. Each layer has a water reservoir with four spouts.

Visitors to the Rijksmuseum find the birdcage (fig. 55), like the violin (fig. 51), one of the most appealing delftware objects in the collection.

It must have been a huge challenge for the factory that won this commission to make a three-dimensional object of this size with so little clay. Fragile objects like this have a tendency to distort or even collapse altogether in the kiln. It has to be regarded as little short of a miracle that in years of use it was never seriously damaged and has consequently survived.

From 1667 onwards, De 3 Vergulde Astonne, which was situated between De Grieksche A and De Metale Pot on De Lange Geer, was jointly owned by Wouter van Eenhoorn and Pieter

55

Birdcage, c. 1685-1700, h. 29 cm, w. 23.5 cm.

The design for this extraordinary birdcage was probably copied from one made of wood and wire. It must have been a huge challenge for the factory to make an object consisting of so much air and so little clay.

56
Vase with cover, c. 1695-1705, attributed to De 3 Vergulde Astonne under the management of Gerrit Kam, h. 49 cm.

The decoration of sprays of flowers and birds placed so close together that the whole thing almost starts to resemble an abstract design was a huge success for Delft and remained in fashion for a very long time.

57
Tankard, c. 1680-1700, h. 24 cm.

While the clay was still soft, flutings were pressed into it with a piece of dowelling.

Gerritsz Kam. Given Van Eenhoorn's numerous and diverse business interests, it seems likely that Kam ran the company. Kam's son Gerrit acquired sole ownership in two phases and then sold the pottery to his son Pieter in 1700. In the following year, Gerrit and his other son, David, acquired De Paeuw, which was less than a hundred yards away. The monograms GK and PK on objects dating from this period are associated with De 3 Vergulde Astonne, the wares from the other factory were probably usually marked with the name 'Paeuw'. The Kam

family developed a style of their own during this period. Much of their work is completely covered with painted sprays of flowers and birds in all sorts of attitudes. As a rule, the effect of the decoration is more satisfactory on a large surface, as in the case of this tall jar with a cover (fig. 56), than on a smaller object. This style of painting was to be used in Delft for very many years. Executed by less skilled painters, painted rather less painstakingly and with a thicker brush, and consequently cheaper to produce, millions of vases, jars and tankards were made and sold. It is probable that simple, unpainted objects intended for everyday use accounted for more than half of the output of the Delft factories. Needless to say, very few of these pieces have survived, but occasionally the first owner fitted an object with a metal rim or cover, like this one in silver-gilt, and this increased its value to the extent that it was subsequently treated with greater care and respect (fig. 57). The jug was thrown on the wheel, after which, while the clay was still soft, the potter took a piece of wooden dowelling and marked a groove in it from the upper left to the lower right. He repeated this seven times, creating the impression that giant hands have fluted the body of the jug. The piece acquired its silver-gilt mount in Enkhuizen at the end of the 17th century.

Twenty successful years in a
stagnating economy (1700-1720)

In January 1701, at a special celebratory meal, Adrianus Kocks transferred De Grieksche A to his son Pieter. Pieter was able to run the factory for only two years. After his death in May 1703, his widow, Johanna van der Heul, decided to carry on with the business herself. She was to run the factory with great success for almost twenty years. Gerrit Pietersz Kam also saw to it around 1700 that his two sons, Pieter and David, each acquired a renowned Delft pottery, so that the third generation of the Kam family could also play their part in the trade. After the de facto bankruptcy of Rochus Hoppesteijn, Het Oude Moriaenshooft and Het Jonge Moriaenshooft fell back to occupy more modest positions. De Metale Pot grew and flourished under Lambertus van Eenhoorn's management.

Many technical and artistic innovations were introduced in Delft around 1680 and again in the 1690s. A great many of the best pieces must have been made in these boom years. This period of prosperity continued into the 18th century, but the market for the wares gradually became more limited. In consequence, it became harder to maintain a high level of production of fine, beautifully decorated luxury items, and this in turn reduced the need to continually improve and innovate in terms of the technology and execution.

The dish (fig. 58) is marked with the monogram PAK, which has been associated since about 1940 with Pieter Adriaensz Kocks and his widow, in short with De Grieksche A, in the first quarter of the 18th century. The style of decoration on the dish is typical of the early part of the 18th century. A dish like this was obviously never meant to be eaten off, it is purely ornamental. The border of the dish has been painted using what is known as the reserve technique. This means that it is not the figures, in this case deer, dogs and children between foliate scrolls, but the background that is painted, so that the decoration stands out in white against a dark surround. It is a time-consuming and costly manner of painting that has to be done with great care, and it can make a border like this appear rather stiff. Jannetje van Straten and her son Rochus Hoppesteijn of Het Moriaenshooft probably set the tone in Delft in

The objects were new
and very colourful.

58

Dish, c. 1705-1715, attributed
to De Grieksche A under the
management of the widow of
Pieter Kocks, diam. 39 cm.

The fireplace in this old Dutch
interior, painted on the right
in the well of the dish, has
17th-century dimensions, some
150 to 175 centimetres high.
A row of plates and bowls and
a dish are arranged on the protruding ledge at the base of the
chimneybreast. And dishes like
this were also proudly displayed
elsewhere in the house, on the
wainscot. A wickerwork cradle
stands in the centre of the room.
The mother of the newborn is
surrounded by three children
ranging in age from about three
to seven. Their father is just
about to open the lower part
of the door.

59 >

Vase with cover, c. 1695-1700,
attributed to De Grieksche A
under the management of
Adrianus Kocks, h. 31 cm.

Colourful Japanese pieces were
so sought-after in Europe that
De Grieksche A was making
accurate copies even before
1700 so that people could make
up sets.

the 1680s in terms of the use of colour,
but they were certainly not the only
entrepreneurs who had come up with
that idea. With a very few exceptions,
however, their competitors restricted
their palettes to green, yellow, purple
and blue, which were easy to fire in the
glaze at about 950 degrees Celsius.
Evidently the occasional potter found
this range of colours inadequate; for
the time being, though, they did not
adopt the rather laborious technique
used by Godtling and Het Moriaenshooft. In the second half of the 1690s,
one or more of the factories succeeded
in developing a red and a black paint
that could withstand the temperature
of the glost firing. This technical inno-

vation made the polychrome painted
Delft faience of the years around 1700
one of the high points of the history of
European ceramics. A wonderful selection of decorative objects and high
quality wares intended for use has been
preserved, only a proportion of which
are marked. As far as the marked pieces
are concerned, two factories come to
the fore: De Roos and De Metale Pot.
Nevertheless, other potteries also produced fine work at the beginning of
the 18th century. There are for example
marked pieces known to have been
produced by De Grieksche A (fig. 59)
during Adrianus Kocks's time – up to
1701 – and a number bearing his son's
marks. After a few years, however, the

59A
Much of the Japanese porcelain was adapted to suit European tastes and intended for a European clientele. The Japanese porcelain painters borrowed decorations in the form of scenes in foliate cartouches from Delft faience.

widow of Pieter Kocks would move her company's technical and artistic ambitions in a different direction (see pp. 124-125).
Lambertus van Eenhoorn, owner of De Metale Pot since 1691, had the products of this pottery marked with his initials LVE. Not every painter will have painted the monogram in exactly the same way and it is possible that one of the bars of the E might have been forgotten every now and then, sometimes making a monogram like this open to different interpreta-

Dish, c. 1705-1720, attributed to De Roos under the management of Dammas Hoffdijck, diam. 48 cm.

This dish might almost have been made in China. However, the Delft version is more lavishly decorated and is much glossier than the Chinese original. The fact that the decoration did not run during firing was a technical feat.

tions. Since the first serious publications about Delft faience in the 19th century, there has been an ongoing debate about the attribution of the monograms LVE, LVF and LV to Lambertus van Eenhoorn or to Louwijs Victoor, owner of De Dobbelde Schenckan. Extraordinarily little is known about the earlier output of this latter company, in contrast to the achievements of De Metale Pot. It is therefore unlikely that De Dobbelde Schenckan played a prominent role in

the development of the technically advanced colour palette that came into being in Delft around 1700.

This jar with a cover (p. 107, fig. 59) is probably the last survivor of a set that originally consisted of five, or even seven jars and vases. The painter in De Grieksche A used as his example a Japanese pot that had been painted in Arita in *Kakiemon* style, but was intended for a European clientele. We know this because the decoration was contained in foliate cartouches, so that

61

Set of vases, c. 1695-1715,
h. 80 cm (jar), h. 58.5 cm
(goblet), h. 57 cm (vase).

The different shapes in this set
of vases are all octagonal and
ribbed. The painter divided the
bellies of the jar and the vases
into eight compartments; the
bulbous bodies of the flasks
were divided into four to allow
the pattern to cover the full
width. The pattern of colourful
sprays of flowers, completely
filling the space, was known as
'cashmere' after the fine woollen
fabric from India, which was
often woven in a similar design.

this piece would have appealed primarily to European tastes (fig. 59A).
The decoration of the large dish
(fig. 60), which is signed *Roos* in full,
the mark of the pottery of the same
name, is derived from the *famille verte*
porcelain that was imported from
China until the end of the 17th century. The painter used all the colours
available to him, including the difficult
red and black. By giving the dish an

additional layer of transparent lead
glaze all over, the maker has achieved
a superb shine. This has also made the
colours appear fresher and more vivid.
In the mid 19th century, collectors in
Europe developed a keen appreciation
of the old earthenware from Delft.
These objects, which until then had
led an unloved existence as expensive
tableware that had gone out of date,
suddenly became sought-after collec-

tors' items. During this period some of the shapes and decorations were given names that often had nothing to do with the original background of the design itself, but rather reflected something in the everyday life of the collectors of the time. A particular pattern of colourful sprays of flowers, for instance, completely filling the space on ribbed vases and jars, was known as 'cashmere' after the fine woollen cashmere shawls from India that were popular during this period. The set of five vases (fig. 61), in which the covered jar is eighty centimetres tall, is one of the finest ensembles in this style to have been preserved. When the heirs of Baron van den Bogaerde auctioned the contents of Heeswijk Castle near Den Bosch at the end of 19th century, the Rijksmuseum decided to do everything possible to keep this set for the Netherlands. It cost almost eight thousand guilders, a huge sum at that time. It is not clear why a set of vases like this, which would have been very expensive for the pottery to make in terms of design and moulds, remained unmarked. As far as the picture of the industry we are now trying to build up is concerned, it is a great shame. By composing this set of a single covered jar, flanked by two goblet-shaped vases and two flasks in the shape of a calabash, the designer has created a beautiful rhythm. We do not know whether all sets of this size were conceived as pieces for display on top of a cupboard or on a sideboard. In Friesland large sets of Japanese porcelain were often displayed on broad window sills.

In the second half of the 17th century, people in Europe started to drink tea and then coffee and chocolate. Need-less to say, new utensils were needed for these exotic beverages. The factories in Delft seldom invented new shapes; instead, responding to the wishes of their prospective buyers, they usually took as their examples models in other materials, such as objects in brass and silver, or porcelain import-ed from China. This type of teapot (fig. 62) has a handle inspired by bam-boo, and the painter has also incor-porated bamboo and Japanese plum blossom in the decoration. The cof-feepot (fig. 63) is painted all over with a design of flower sprigs and birds that is like the exuberant decoration on the set of vases (fig. 61).

As we have already seen (p. 97), Lambertus van Eenhoorn was, as far as we know, the first pottery-owner in Delft to employ a sculptor to work on design. The pieces with polychrome decoration that are marked with his

62
Teapot, c. 1695-1715, h. 12 cm.

The handle is inspired by bamboo, and the painter has also incorporated bamboo and Japanese plum blossom in the decoration, giving an Oriental feel to this object, which was still completely new to the European consumer.

63
Coffeepot, c. 1695-1715,
attributed to De Metale Pot
under the management of
Lambertus van Eenhoorn,
h. 25.5 cm.

New utensils had to be developed for serving the then new
beverages of tea, chocolate and
coffee. The Delft potteries
usually looked to examples in
metal to get ideas. Brightly
coloured decoration meant
that the finished piece looked
very different from the original
silver or copper pot.

64 (pp. 114-115)
Pair of cachepots, c. 1695-1715,
attributed to De Metale Pot
under the management of
Lambertus van Eenhoorn,
h. 38 cm.

The decoration has been subordinated to the shape, which has
been assembled from individual
elements.

monogram clearly reveal that the company also employed an experienced
craftsman in this field too. De Metale
Pot played an important – if not the
most important – role in the development of new colours and colour combinations, and in the composition of
new decorative schemes that would
incorporate the new *grand feu* colours.
For the coffeepot (fig. 63), De Metale

Pot's modeller designed a mould for
half of the shape; the two identical
halves were then joined with a semi-
liquid mixture of clay and water,
known as slip. The long spout, the
handle and the three feet were added
last. The two large decorative cachepots (fig. 64) must have given Van
Eenhoorn's designer a lot more to
think about. The foot and the top

5
ooler with two flasks,
1695-1715, attributed to
e Metale Pot under the
management of Lambertus van
enhoorn, h. 21.5 cm, w. 31 cm,
. 25 cm (cooler), h. 31.5 cm,
. 16 cm (flasks).

he cooler is an example of the
ew style that the Frenchman
aniel Marot brought to the
etherlands. With an object in
equent use, as this was, it is
ttle short of a miracle that the
agile flasks have survived in
uch good condition.

of the flaring pot were thrown, as was a perforated inset that cannot be seen in the illustration. A mould was made for the piece in between. The four elements must then have been joined with slip, after which the whole thing had to be left to dry. The various leaves in relief that decorate the pots were pressed in a mould separately, removed at the leather-hard stage and then attached to the surface of the vase with slip. The potter, the moulder and the finisher must have put many hours of work into it. After they had been fired and the glaze applied, the pots were painted with the utmost care in strong, bright colours in line with the latest fashion. The cooler with the two

surviving flasks (fig. 65) is another example of the new style that Daniel Marot had brought to the Netherlands, with the cartouches filled with foliate motifs, the garlands of flowers, the borders resembling twisted rope, and above all the regular structure of the decoration. This piece was thrown first and then shaped into an oval, after which a base, cut into an oval, was suspended in it to keep the whole thing in the right shape.

As we described at the beginning of this chapter (see p. 63), the furnishing of the domestic interior underwent a metamorphosis in this period, and table settings were also modified in line with new customs. We do not

6
wo figurines, c. 1700-1715,
ttributed to De Metale Pot
nder the management of
ambertus van Eenhoorn,
. 17.5 cm.

imilar figurines of boys on
linths exist playing a *viola
a gamba*, a hurdy-gurdy, or
agpipes, or simply standing,
aning on a stick. Whole series
f these little figures could be
rdered, and they could be
upplied, according to the
ustomer's wishes, in blue or
olychrome faience, decorated
n the glaze with enamel
olours, and even in red
oneware.

67
Flower vase, c. 1705-1715,
h. 20 cm, w. 21 cm.

The flat style with six or eight
spouts and two identical animals
or mythological creatures as
handles is one of the best-known
Delft creations. They are usually
described as tulip or hyacinth
vases, but they look equally
superb filled with other blooms.

know precisely what function figurines
like the boy playing a violin on a plinth
(fig. 66) had in the interior: on étagères
against the wall or as an ornament to
dress up the table.

The small flower vase (fig. 67) has only
a painter's mark – IH – but judging by
its design, it could very well have come
from De Metale Pot. In this factory the
monogram LVE was often accompanied by size and (possibly) decoration
codes and sometimes also by a painter's signature.

By the end of the 17th century, the potteries were so skilled in the technique
of keeping the tin glaze sufficiently
stable during firing that the decoration did not run but the finished piece
still had a high shine that they were
prepared to take risks and experiment.
Some of the factories coloured the
glaze blue, olive green and even black
through and through. A decoration
was then painted on this coloured
ground in one or more colours. In
Italy and in Nevers, in France, faience

68

Jug, c. 1695-1715, h. 16.5 cm.

A glaze coloured all the way through was among the new ideas that some of the potteries came up with towards the end of the 17th century. The painting technique was adapted to the new ground; the decoration consisted of thickly applied areas of colour.

69

Teapot, c. 1695-1715, attributed to Het Jonge Moriaenshooft under the management of Lieve van Dalen, h. 10 cm.

The new owner of the Hoppe-steijn family pottery concentrated, among other things, on a brownish-green ground, which was then decorated in yellow.

makers had previously covered objects with an opaque blue or yellow glaze, but it was in Delft that they succeeded for the first time in painting a finely executed decoration on this blue which did not run during firing. It can be seen from the breaking of the white areas just how difficult it is to stop the decoration from slumping into the glaze (fig. 68). The new owner of Het Jonge Moriaenshooft, Lieve van Dalen, concentrated on a brownish-green ground, which was then decorated in different ways in his factory. This little teapot (fig. 69) is covered relatively simply with scattered yellow flowers.

70

Oval bowl, c. 1695-1715,
attributed to De Metale Pot
under the management of
Lambertus van Eenhoorn,
h. 5 cm, w. 24.5 cm, d. 20.5 cm.

The endeavour to cover earthenware with a black ground was
probably a response to Chinese
and Japanese lacquer work. The
Delft potteries' success in doing
this was a significant technical
and artistic achievement.

Lambertus van Eenhoorn's De Metale
Pot also played a prominent role in
the development of coloured grounds,
since it was most likely there that a
deep black ground was developed.
The colour black was based in part
on manganese oxide, an oxide that
reacts aggressively with other colours.
Technically speaking, executing part
of a polychrome painting in black was
usually not a problem, but it required
tremendous technical knowledge and
skill to apply a decoration on a black
ground. The challenge to produce
pieces covered in a black ground was
probably prompted by lacquer work
imported from China and Japan:
wooden objects painted dark brown
or black and covered with coats of
highly glossy lacquer. Faience with
a black ground must have had the
same expensive aura as these exotic

Oriental pieces. The oval ribbed bowl
(fig. 70) is a fine example of the extraordinary technical and artistic achievements at De Metale Pot. The bright
colours of the decoration, borrowed
from Chinese porcelain, stand out
beautifully against the black background. To get the dark and transparent colours to show up against
the black background and at the same
time to restrict the reactivity of the
manganese oxide in the black, the
painter has added small white areas
between the ground and the colour.
The black glaze was also used at De
Grieksche A, just down the road, but
in a different and technically much
simpler way. This little teapot (fig. 71),
which is marked with the monogram
PAK, for Pieter Adriaensz Kocks, was
painted in the traditional manner on
the white glaze. Then the painter filled

71

Teapot, c. 1705-1720, attributed
to De Grieksche A under the
management of the widow of
Pieter Kocks, h. 13 cm.

In this case the design is not
painted on a black ground; the
black is part of the polychrome
decoration.

in the white background in black, working very carefully around the polychrome decoration. The black painted objects from this factory seem to be less inspired, in part because of the limited use of colour, but it was this firm which, soon after 1700, specialized in a different, equally exceptional technique based on enamels.

One particular type of Japanese Arita porcelain must have been exceptionally popular in the Netherlands around 1700. The Dutch evidently wanted porcelain with decoration all over, where the blue was applied under the glaze and the other colours, like enamels, on the glaze. This type, *Imari* porcelain, has always been very well represented in Dutch collections. It is consequently not surprising that

the Delft potters tried to capture part of this sector of the market. The great majority of the Japanese exports consisted of dishes and covered jars, which were combined with vases to make sets. The Delft factories focused on shapes that were not being supplied, or not in enough different sizes, by the Japanese porcelain makers.

The shape of the round box (fig. 72) is derived from a wooden tub or pail, made from staves like a barrel. In the decoration of narrow panels there is a rhythm moving from light to dark, so that four pieces create a harmonious whole. This technique was probably borrowed from large Japanese bowls with heavy lobes, each of which had a panel of this kind. Because the decoration of the cover is painted over the whole surface, it doesn't really go

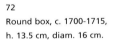

72
Round box, c. 1700-1715,
h. 13.5 cm, diam. 16 cm.

The shape of the box is reminiscent of a wooden pail or a barrel, made from staves held together with hoops of metal or stripped willow.

73
Bowl with cover, c. 1710-1720,
h. 28 cm, diam. 26 cm.

The regular division of the
space, the straight bands with
which the flowers and the landscape are separated from each
other and the full decoration rob
this large bowl of any Japanese
feel despite the *Imari* colours.

with the box. All in all, however, an extremely useful object that looked very Japanese was created for the Dutch consumer of the day.
The model for bowls like this (fig. 73) with a Chinese lion as the knop on the cover is a faithful imitation of porcelain bowls that were ordered in Japan by the Dutch East India Company especially for the Dutch market. By dividing the surface into four with blue bands, the painter was going back to earlier examples. Dividing the face of a jar, a flask

or a vase into sections was not unusual in Delft in the second half of the 17th century. Despite the *Imari* colours, the regular division of the surface and the straight bands rob the piece of any Japanese feel. The decoration, a flower still life that fills the whole area interspersed with a water landscape, must have been adapted from large *Imari* dishes. In this group of delftware there is seldom any question of out and out copying; it would be more accurate to describe it as an interaction, where the

74
Teapot, c. 1720-1730, h. 15 cm.

The handle is attached to the pot with two gargoyles, which were usually used in Delft as the spouts on flower vases.

amenable to being modelled and relief work on an object can stand out really sharply provided the glaze is not applied too thickly. Nevertheless, the Delft potteries almost always opted for painted decoration. This is what people were used to, and a beautifully painted object like this may perhaps also have conveyed a greater sense of luxury. Parts of the pot were painted blue first, possibly with the intention of decorating the fields in *Imari* style. Evidently there was a change of mind and gold was applied on the blue, but the open areas were filled with *Kakiemon* motifs, a style that was very sought-after towards the end of the 1720s.

One factory in Delft is at the forefront when it comes to the extent and the artistic standard of this sort of faience with a Japanese feel to it – De Grieksche A under the management of Pieter Kocks and, even more, when his widow Johanna van der Heul was running it. Very many of the best pieces bear the mark that was used at De Grieksche A at this time: PAK. The firm was able to supply complete dinner services in this style to the European elite. The plate (fig. 75) comes from a service made for Frederick I, Elector of Brandenburg and King of Prussia. The design is made up of the monarch's coat of arms, surrounded by the chain of the Order of the Black Eagle, and alternately the crowned monogram FR (Fredericus Rex), the black crowned eagle of Prussia and the red crowned eagle and shield of Brandenburg. Everything possible was done to emphasize the importance of the new monarch. All the usual colours have already been incorporated in this early

eventual Delft result would have looked Oriental to the consumers of the day and would not have been out of place in an interior with genuine *Imari* porcelain.

In this little teapot (fig. 74), the Delft potter has used examples from Japan and China and combined them with inventions of his own to make something completely new. The colours that have been used make it look very Japanese. The shape of the little pot is borrowed from a Chinese example in red stoneware or possibly in the white undecorated Chinese porcelain known as *blanc de chine*. The Delft modeller has made two changes, the handle is attached to the pot with two gargoyles, also used in Delft as the spouts of flower holders, and the faces are not decorated in relief. Faience is extremely

75

Plate, c. 1702-1705, attributed to De Grieksche A under the management of the widow of Pieter Kocks, diam. 22 cm.

Frederick I, Elector of Brandenburg, had himself crowned King of Prussia in Koningsbergen (Kaliningrad) in 1701. This plate was part of the service that was ordered in Delft shortly after his coronation.

example: blue in the glaze, and red, burgundy, green, gold and black on the glaze. Johanna van der Heul must have regarded *Imari*-style faience as an important and lucrative market, and one that she very much wanted to

protect. Following the departure of two of her pottery assistants to another company, on 14 December 1713 a statement was made in front of a notary by 'Mistress Johanna van der Heul, widow of the late Master Pieter Kocx and potter in the porcelain factory De Grieksche A in this town, party of the first part' and four named pottery assistants, among them Adriaen van Rijsselbergh, the parties of the second part, in which they let it be known that 'for so long as the party of the first part [Johanna van der Heul] carries on the trade and manufacture of porcelain at the aforesaid pottery De Griekse A, they will continue to work there and specifically will practise the art of painting and firing gold on the Delft porcelain, without leaving said shop or practising the aforesaid art of painting

76

Chocolate cup, c. 1702-1715, attributed to De Grieksche A under the management of the widow of Pieter Kocks, h. 7.5 cm, diam. 6.5 cm.

When it was first introduced into Europe and for the next hundred and fifty years, cocoa was so high in fat that it did not dissolve easily in hot water or hot milk. Tall cups, which made it possible to stir the contents vigorously, were consequently designed for hot chocolate.

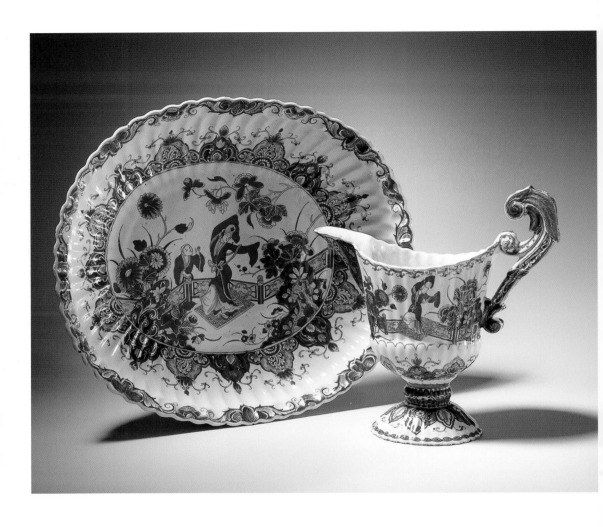

77
Ewer and bowl, c. 1702-1715,
attributed to De Grieksche A
under the management of
the widow of Pieter Kocks,
h. 26.5 cm (ewer), w. 40.5 cm,
d. 34.5 cm (bowl).

Around 1700, forks were added
to the usual table cutlery of
knives and spoons, and people
were no longer expected to eat
with their hands. Ewer and bowl
sets for use at the table then
essentially lost their function.

gold on Delft porcelain at any other
shop'. In the first twenty years of
the 18th century many thousands of
superb pieces must have been painted
in this style at De Grieksche A.
The tall cup (fig. 76) decorated with a
cockerel is a relatively simple object. It
has traditionally been assumed that tall
cups like this were designed as beakers
for hot chocolate. The imposing ewer
and bowl set, in contrast, may well have
been intended exclusively for ceremoni-

al use (fig. 77). In the late 17th century,
when the use of forks at table, and not
just spoons and knives, became fairly
general, it was no longer necessary for
people to wash their hands after every
course, and ewer and bowl sets at the
table fell into disuse. The shape of the
basin and the jug is European, as is
the decoration, except for the Chinese
dancing girl. It is only the colours
that give the set a Japanese feel. The
tankard (fig. 78) acquired its silver

78
Tankard, c. 1702-1710,
attributed to De Grieksche A
under the management of
the widow of Pieter Kocks,
h. 25.4 cm, diam. 16.4 cm.

The decoration featuring a
cellist and the silver cover would
indicate that this piece was made
to order. It is unlikely that beer
was ever drunk from it.

78A
The engraving which the
Delft painter used as his
example for the decoration
of the tankard.

79
Jar with cover, c. 1710-1722,
attributed to De Grieksche A
under the management of
the widow of Pieter Kocks,
h. 44 cm.

This ornamental piece was
probably part of a set of three
jars and two vases.

0

ish, c. 1715-1722, attributed
o De Grieksche A under the
nanagement of the widow of
ieter Kocks, diam. 40 cm.

uropa is seduced by the Greek
od Zeus, who had disguised
imself as a bull. The painter
sed a hundred-year-old print
r this mythological scene.

cover in Rotterdam, probably in 1709. The highly unusual decoration featuring a cellist might indicate that this piece was made to order. The painter in Delft used an engraving by B. Picart after I.C. Weigel dating from about 1705.

The covered jar (fig. 79) boasts incomparably lavish and refined painting. Here again, it is only because of the colours that the piece makes a Japanese impression. The two women in front of a dignitary on one side, the woman making music and three men in a garden on the other sides are derived from the Chinese porcelain of the period. This ornamental piece was probably part of a set of three jars and two vases (see pp. 110-111, fig. 61), none of the other pieces of which appear to have survived. Whereas the painter had chosen a contemporary print for the tankard (fig. 78), for the dish (fig. 80) he used a print from the illustrations

81
Pair of small jugs with covers,
c. 1723-1730, attributed to
Adriaen van Rijsselbergh,
h. 16 cm.

The asymmetry of the
decoration is very Japanese.

by Hendrick Goltzius for an edition of the *Metamorphoses* by the classical author Ovid. An engraving like this, depicting 'Europa seduced by Jupiter disguised as a bull' was probably just one of the many examples and pouncing stencils kept in stock in the factory. The fact that a hundred-year-old print was being used was evidently not perceived as a problem. These three pieces, all of which radiate refined elegance, must have been painted by the best craftsman in the company. Perhaps it was Adriaen van Rijsselbergh, one of the gilders mentioned by name in the notarial deed.

In 1722 Johanna van der Heul sold the pottery. Shortly afterwards, no longer contractually bound, Adriaen van Rijsselbergh decided to set up in business for himself. A number of pieces in the style of De Grieksche A, but with the monogram AR, have survived, all of which must date from the 1720s. The manner of painting is generally a little freer than on the pieces from De Grieksche A. The pair of small covered jugs (fig. 81) is a good example of the style that Van Rijsselbergh had developed in his later years. The asymmetry of the decoration is very Japanese; on the right a dark section with a rendition of an unrolled scroll painting borrowed from *Imari* porcelain and on the left an open area with no more than a branch and some birds. The handle and the separate covers have holes for a pewter or silver hinge.

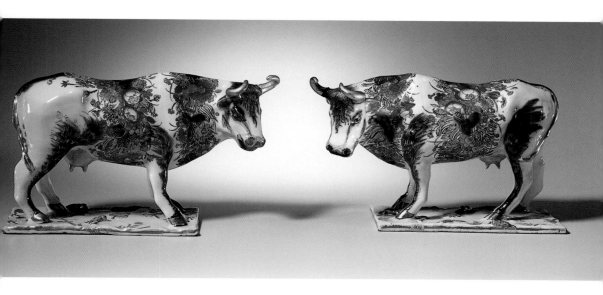

82
Pair of cows, c. 1720-1730,
h. 15 cm, w. 24 cm.

They could scarcely be more
Dutch: two well-built cows
decorated with flowers. The
colour scheme is derived from
Japanese *Imari* porcelain.

These were never put on and so the
jugs, not really much use because of
this, were put away in a cupboard,
where they remained to survive virtually unscathed. The set of cows
(fig. 82) is related to Japanese porcelain
only in the use of colour. Ornaments
like this may have had a specific function – to decorate a dining table for a
special occasion. In everyday use they
would have stood on a mantelpiece or
cupboard, or in a glass and porcelain
cabinet.

The economic prosperity of the nation
suffered a downturn after 1700, and
the faience industry was no exception.
To call a halt at 1720, as has been done
in this book, is rather arbitrary. In the
first twenty years of the 18th century
there was a notable shift from large
quantities of high quality wares with
few simple pieces, dictated by compe-

tition, towards much less carefully
designed objects with relatively simple
decoration. In the end the factories
produced very few really elegant wares
that demonstrated the high technical
and artistic standard of which the Delft
potters were capable. It is these latter
wares on which the collection in the
Rijksmuseum focuses. These changes
continued until 1724, a year in which
the potteries took drastic measures.

A deep recession with technical and artistic highlights (1720-1750)

In political terms little changed in the Netherlands in the first half of the 18th century. The nation had sunk back into a position that befitted its small size. A small country, with a relatively large population, most of whom lived in the towns and cities. The Netherlands was no longer on an equal footing with European states like England and France, and was slowly but surely being overtaken by a rising power like the German state of Prussia. In economic terms, too, the country had lost its superior position. So much money had been earned in the 17th century, however, that Amsterdam could still be Europe's banker. Life in the Netherlands was expensive. This was true of luxury products, but certainly also of the basic necessities of life. As a result, wages in the 18th century were usually too high for the Netherlands to be able to compete effectively with other countries on the basis of price, and this applied to a great many products. In the 1730s, agriculture was doing neither well nor badly. In the livestock farming sector there were repeated outbreaks of cattle plague, and these epidemics devastated the national herd several

times between 1730 and 1750. Where industrial crops were grown, the farmers were essentially unaffected by these crises, and in the Zaan region, a rural area with well-developed industry, the people were actually prosperous and had money to spend.

After years of ups and downs in the faience industry, the economic situation changed so drastically for the Delft potteries that they found themselves compelled to take radical steps. In order to tackle the problem of sales, in 1724 the pottery owners agreed to a joint restriction of production volumes, which they set out in a deed before a notary. The motivation given was '... on the one hand the flourishing State in which the potteries in this Town have been, counting twenty, thirty and more Years back, and on the other the poor State in which the same are Presently'. In order to rein in overproduction and counter competition between them, the pottery owners made a number of agreements. Every year all the factories would be shut down for the whole of the month of January, discounts for merchants according to the length of the sup-

Plates for everyday use at table were the mainstay of the industry during this period.

plier's credit were no longer to exceed two percent, and a minimum price was fixed for a whole range of products. At the same time the pottery owners decided to introduce a costly system to combat overproduction: poorly performing companies would be bought out. Consequently, between 1726 and 1753 six smaller potteries were bought up by the association of pottery owners and then closed down: De Ham in 1726, China in 1740, Het Hooge Huys in 1741, Rouaan and De Vier Romeynse Helden, both in 1742, and finally, in 1753, Het Gecroond Porceleyn. All the plant and equipment in these factories was put out of action permanently, and it was ruled that the trade of potter could never again be carried on in these premises.

One of the reasons for these far-reaching measures was the successful introduction of Chinese porcelain with decorations in *famille rose* and *Imari* colours. In the first twenty years of the 18th century, sales potential outside the Netherlands had been reduced by the establishment in other countries of dozens of competing faience potteries. But it was the rise of Saxon porcelain in Germany, specifically designed for the European elite, which really made things difficult for even the best Delft factories.

In only a few cases did the potteries that had played a leading role in the period after 1680 change hands after 1700. As a rule, the businessmen, their widows or their heirs had continued to run the businesses. Around 1720 this situation altered. The old guard who had reaped the benefits of the 17th-century growth and, by introducing new ideas, had managed to maintain

a reasonable standard of prosperity, had had their day. Lambertus van Eenhoorn died in 1721, and in 1724 his widow made his pottery, De Metale Pot, over to Cornelis Koppens. Johanna van der Heul, widow of Pieter Kocks since 1703, had sold De Grieksche A to Jacob van der Kool in 1722. The story of the Kam family's factory, De 3 Vergulde Astonne, was a rather sad one. After the death of Pieter Kam, the death of his widow Maria van der Kloot and two years later of their only daughter, Maria's father inherited the pottery. Anthonij van der Kloot was a tobacco merchant, so he probably left the day to day running of the business to someone else from the outset. It may have been Gerardus Nahuys, who lodged in Van der Kloot's house, who took on the management role in the company (fig. 89). In 1722, Nahuys moved to Utrecht and the pottery was sold to Zacharias Dextra. As to De Witte Starre and De Roos, both of which belonged to Jacobus de Lange and Dammas Hoffdijck, De Lange had bought out his partner in De Witte Starre in 1711. Together they sold De Roos in about 1713, after which Hoffdijck retired from business. De Lange died in 1716, but his widow Francina van der Eijck managed to run the pottery successfully (fig. 88). In 1723, one day before she died, she sold the company to her nephew Cornelis Brouwer. David Kam, whose father Gerrit Kam had bought De Paeuw for him in 1701, died in 1719 having managed the business profitably; his widow continued to run the company for another six years. In 1725 their children sold the company to a certain Jan Wessels who, after splitting off a parcel of land, sold it on to Jan

The professional association to which the pottery owners had to belong was the Guild of St Luke. In the course of the 17th century, the position of the pottery owners strengthened vis a vis the fine artists in Delft. A sandstone garland made up of jars, jugs and plates was mounted on the wall of the guildhall.

Verhagen in 1729. The latter probably had a sound background as a faience painter (fig. 91). A few months after his death in 1739 his widow sold the pottery to Jacobus de Milde. Between 1720 and 1725 the Van Eenhoorn family, including brothers-in-law, cousins and nephews, and the Kam family, who had played a prominent part in the business for three generations, suddenly disappeared as an influential factor in the Delft faience industry. The background of the new generation of owners is not always entirely clear. Zacharias Dextra was originally a jeweller. His second marriage to Johanna van Ruyven in 1721 probably

made him so wealthy that he could afford to buy an important faience factory. When Jacob van der Kool and Cornelis Brouwer acquired the two highly renowned companies, De Grieksche A and De Witte Starre respectively, each sold his smaller pottery: Het Oude Moriaenshooft and De Porceleyne Schotel. In the preceding ten years these companies had grown and flourished under their management. Van der Kool came from a family of potters of the second rank. His father had run De Drie Porceleyne Flessies since 1675. The elder son, Willem, succeeded him in 1702. Jacob, as the second son, must have worked

83
Tea caddy, c. 1715-1725,
attributed to De Grieksche A
under the management of
the widow of Pieter Kocks,
h. 17.5 cm, w. 11.2 cm,
d. 7.1 cm.

The motif of the bird with a
long tail, sitting in a ring, is
also common on Japanese
pieces with Dutch decoration.

with him in the business until Willem was able to buy his brother out and Jacob was in a position to afford a company of his own, Het Oude Moriaenshooft. The Van der Kool family rose in the trade over the course of fifty years. When De Grieksche A, the most prestigious Delft faience pottery, came on to the market, it was Jacob who bought it, possibly with the assistance of his wife Cornelia van der Willigen. She received an advance on her inheritance of fourteen thousand guilders, possibly as early as 1722. The standard of the original family firm, De Drie Porceleyne Flessies, was also to improve during the reign of the second generation (fig. 97).

In economic terms, the year 1724 marked the end of an era that had

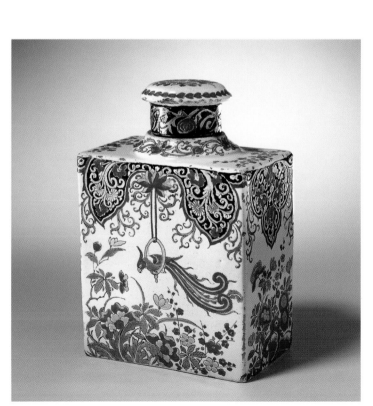

started well for the old generation of pottery owners. When business began to go badly, they kept their heads above water with great ingenuity in the hope that the tide would turn. The new generation of manufacturers were prepared to face the truth and, in 1724, took the steps to limit output that we discussed above. From the artistic point of view neither the cut-off point of 1720 we use here nor the year 1724 is a clear demarcation line. Even when times were not as good as they had been, economically speaking, there was still a limited market for expensively produced items. In the first twenty years of the 18th century, with their faience decorated in *Imari* colours, Johanna van der Heul and her 'gilders' at De Grieksche A had shown the way forward for elaborate and beautifully decorated objects. And so the standard of some of the decoration remained high even after 1720.

The development of new colours and shades that could be applied on top of the glaze increased the options and stimulated the imagination. Painters even started to apply the whole of the decoration on the glaze, with what were known as enamel paints. These pigments could be fired in an enamelling kiln at about 600 degrees Celsius. For this reason, the literature refers to *petit feu*, and sometimes to enamel colours and the enamelling technique. The demand from the market for the decoration of undecorated Japanese porcelain and white or simply decorated Chinese porcelain must have encouraged some Delft companies to specialize in this. After about 1710, these Oriental objects were often decorated in *Kakiemon* style, but very occasionally with

84
Pair of dishes, c. 1720-1730, attributed to Adriaen van Rijsselbergh, diam. 30 cm.

The woman seated side-saddle on a horse, surrounded by warriors with lances and whips, could have stepped straight off a Chinese dish. Van Rijsselbergh adapted the decoration as he saw fit.

European subjects too. The lavishly decorated tea caddy (fig. 83) was probably painted in the same period as the dish (p. 129, fig. 80), the last years of De Grieksche A under Johanna van der Heul. The colours used for the decoration are similar: a great deal of dark red and black. When she sold the factory in 1722, Johanna van der Heul let it be known that she wanted to keep the 'glazed and fired fine porcelain' herself, probably so that she could deal in it on her own account. Under the new owner, Jacob van der Kool, the factory did not work in this technique for very long, or at least there are almost no known marked

pieces. At least one gilder seized his opportunity and left. The sale of De Grieksche A released Adriaen van Rijsselbergh from his contractual obligation to remain with the company. Shortly afterwards, possibly as early as 1723, Van Rijsselbergh started his own studio. It is not known whether he had his own kiln. In 1727 Van Rijsselbergh demanded payment from a merchant, a woman in Amsterdam, for decorating 'porcelain in the very best manner as a gilder'. The pair of dishes (fig. 84) is decorated with a woman seated side-saddle on a horse, surrounded by warriors with lances and whips. One cools her with a large fan. The woman carries

85
Pair of cuspidors, c. 1715-1725,
h. 9 cm, diam. 12 cm.

The gentlemen smoke long
clay pipes to evaluate the
tobacco. The Gouda earthenware factories were famous
for their pipes.

86 >
Plaque, c. 1730-1740, h. 38 cm,
w. 32 cm.

A series of prints after drawings
by Jacopo Amigoni was used
as the example for the biblical
scenes from the Old Testament.
This series was published by
J. Wagner in Venice.

a stringed instrument on her back. The
two sumptuously decorated cuspidors
(fig. 85), spittoons for tobacco, show
gentlemen smoking long Gouda pipes
and assessing the tobacco, and negroes
plucking tobacco leaves and making
them into rolls. The painting of the
European figures with long wigs is
very similar in style to the cello-player
on the tankard (fig. 78). The painter
of these exceptional pieces must have
come from De Grieksche A. It is possible that here, too, the painter was
Adriaen van Rijsselbergh himself.
Plaques with a biblical scene (fig. 86)
are usually difficult to date. A rather
more colourful and lavishly decorated
example in Brussels is marked with the
date 1726. We do not know a great deal
about which companies and studios

painted these sorts of decorations
on white wares, nor for how long the
practice continued. The studios could
function with little in the way of
resources and the owners probably
needed much less operating capital.
Every household had brushes in all
sorts of shapes and sizes. They were
usually made of wood, but smaller
examples that the gentleman or lady
of the house used themselves were
sometimes crafted from more expensive materials like silver or finely
painted china (fig. 87). The backs have
survived as attractive curiosities; in
most cases the bristles have been lost.
The way they are decorated is typical
of a group that is usually dated to the
1725-1740 period. These gracefully
painted objects in the enamel tech-

88 >

Plaque, c. 1715-1720, h. 58.5 cm, w. 47.5 cm.

Evidently people associated the size and shape of 'tea trays' like this with a wooden tray or the top of a folding tea table.

nique (figs. 83-87) accounted for only a small proportion of the output.

The quality of the objects decorated in the *petit feu* or enamel technique is outstanding within delftware as a whole. This is why they have survived and ultimately found their way into the Rijksmuseum's collection. This is also true of the pieces in this collection decorated in blue and polychrome in the *grand feu* technique. All the objects illustrated here are exceptions, occasional pieces, that can be linked to a first owner or a pottery, or that boast a design or decoration that sets them far above the average. However, they give a distorted picture of the Delft faience that was being produced in the period from shortly before 1720 until shortly after 1750. The main output of the twenty-plus working potteries consisted of simply decorated or white wares that graced the tables, living rooms and kitchens of a broad middle class. These were the mainstay of the industry.

The heyday of the Delft faience makers was over, but technically and artistically

they were still capable of doing a great deal. Many of the occasional pieces must have been exceptional even then. An extensive inventory was drawn up for the execution of the will of Francina van der Eijck, owner of De Witte Starre. Her possessions were described room by room: 'front room with parrot and cage', the passage with 'three small Delft porcelain plates in frames', 'two tea trays'. It is possible that the plaque (fig. 88) is one of the 'tea trays' described in the inventory. Large, more or less oval plaques or plaquettes like this were sometimes referred to as tea trays or tea tables. Another similar example is marked with a large star on the back. The domestic scenes are very reminiscent of the work of De Witte Starre and De Roos (see pp. 92-96) dating from the first part of the 18th century. The oak (*eik*) in the coat of arms would also seem to be a reference to the Van der Eijck family name. The piece is lavishly executed with a border in relief. Exceptionally, for a period in the 18th century De Witte Starre employed a carver to make moulds. Augustinus Knollenburgh, 'master

87

Brush back, c. 1725-1735, w. 16 cm.

It is possible that this elegant brush with a shepherd once had a 'pendant', decorated with a shepherdess.

89
Dish, dated 1718, diam. 38.7 cm.

True to tradition, the border is decorated with eight large and eight small compartments filled alternately with flowers and collages of Tao symbols. Interestingly, the Chinese example used in this case was already almost hundred years old.

Carver', was appointed 'potter at De Starre' in 1713. The highly detailed decoration is indicative of a special order, in this case for the owner of the pottery herself.

Anthonij van der Kloot became the owner of De 3 Vergulde Astonne in 1718. Gerardus Nahuys, a talented faience painter who was born in Delfshaven in 1695, was lodging with Van der Kloot at this time. Perhaps Nahuys

made a couple of exceptional pieces in an attempt to impress Van der Kloot (fig. 89). In this dish, which is dated 12-11-1718 on the back and marked with the mirror-image monogram NA AN, he was imitating the Chinese porcelain that had been imported in huge quantities until 1647. There has to have been a particular reason for this, for after seventy years people must surely have regarded this sort of decoration as

0
Dish, dated 1718, diam. 40.5 cm.

Moses holds the tablets of stone
bearing the Ten Commandments.
Below is the Apostles' Creed.
The border refers to three pas-
sages from the New Testament
Romans 8, verses 24 and 25;
Corinthians, verses 12 and 13;
nd Hebrews 11), which are
aken as the texts for sermons
t confirmation services.

old-fashioned. The execution and
the painting are of very high quality.
Nahuys moved to Utrecht, and in
1722 Van der Kloot sold the pottery
to Zacharias Dextra (figs. 101 and
102-104).
The next dish (fig. 90) is an absolutely
typical occasional piece. This dish,
dated as it is, must have been made
as a gift for someone who was being
confirmed.

This object (fig. 91) is part of a group
of dated faience bearing the mark IVH,
with exceptionally full and fine decoration. The dates run from 1723 to 1730.
The IVH monogram was traditionally
attributed to Jan van der Hagen, who
managed Het Jonge Moriaenshooft
on behalf of his father, Cornelis, from
1732 onwards. According to the latest
theories, however, the monogram is
now thought to be that of Jan Verha-

143

91
Dish, dated 1728, attributed to
Jan Verhagen, diam. 39.5 cm.

The decoration on the well
of the dish depicts a peasant
festival against the background
of an inn where the broom has
been hung out – the sign of a
party (when the cat's away the
mice will play). People eat, drink
and dance. Elsewhere a couple
flirts. The scene is in the style of
David Vinckboons after a print
by Pieter Gerwouters dating
from 1608. The print, needless
to say, was not round; it was,
moreover, so small that the
lower part of the scene was left
to the painter's imagination.

92
Mirror frame, dated 1736,
h. 65 cm, w. 54 cm.

The decoration has been done in
the time-consuming and costly
reserve technique, as was customary for very expensive items in
this period. In the cartouches
there are four allegorical female
figures, representing Prudentia
(caution), Justitia (justice),
Caritas (charity) and possibly
Temperantia (moderation). The
painter has used examples from
prints for these female figures,
including one by Crispijn van
de Passe dating from the early
17th century. The designer was
obviously not at all concerned
that this example was more
than a century old.

gen, who owned De Paeuw between
1729 and 1739. This would at the
same time explain why the series
stops around 1730. As the owner of
the factory, Verhagen would no longer
have had time for this sort of work.
This mirror frame (fig. 92) must have
been an exceptional piece even for the
most important potteries. Even in
comparison with the bases of the huge
tulip vases dating from the end of the
17th century the frame is so large that
it has to be considered an amazing
technical feat that it did not crack
during firing. The design was probably derived from an example in silver.
When the frame was shaped, part of
the decoration was raised in relief, a
technique in Delft faience that is actually only found in products made by

De Metale Pot and De Witte Starre.
These companies are known to have
employed carvers to design models
and make forms (figs. 52, 64, 88).
The inventory of the estate of the
widow of Cornelis Brouwer – who
owned De Witte Starre from 1723
to 1738 – lists a mirror with a 'Delft
porcelain frame' in 'the large front
room'. It is possible that the exceptional piece in the Rijksmuseum was
made in De Witte Starre in 1736 as
a tribute to the then owner, who had
run the company for twelve and a half
years. This could also explain the
absence of the factory mark.
In 1739 Jacobus de Milde became the
new owner of De Paeuw. He bought
an existing company with a workforce,
stock and traditions. The design for

93

Dressing table basket, dated 1740, attributed to De Paeuw under the management of Jacobus de Milde, h. 15.5 cm.

Elegant and slender, decorated in part with a pierced lace pattern. Two handles are to pick the little basket up; the third is to hang it on the wall.

93A

The decoration inside the basket reveals its use: a receptacle on a dressing table.

this little basket (fig. 93), which is marked 'Paauw', was already seventy years old in 1740. The sides were thrown and then pressed into an oval and the bottom was wedged in, after which simple little feet and the typical ceramic handles twisted to resemble cord were attached. A pierced decoration resembling lace was then painstakingly applied. In comparison with 17th-century examples, the model has become a little slimmer and – almost self-evidently – the decoration has been adapted somewhat to the fashion of the day.

The products that can be attributed to De Grieksche A and De Metale Pot, notwithstanding their new owners, Jacob van der Kool and Cornelis Koppens, are still entirely imbued with the spirit of their predecessors, the Kocks and Van Eenhoorn families. The figurine (fig. 94) must have been designed at De Grieksche A at some time around 1730. The decoration of the low plinth is typical of the 1730s. Developing new figures and the neces-

94

Figurine, c. 1725-1740, attributed to De Grieksche A under the management of Jacob van der Kool, h. 23 cm.

The idea of a boy pulling a thorn out of his foot goes back to the *Spinario*, a statue of classical antiquity that was one of the sights of Rome in the 17th century.

sary moulds to make them was a complicated and expensive process. Once a factory had a design, there was a tendency to use it for a very long time. With the aid of a mould it was possible to go on making copies more or less ad infinitum. It is consequently all the

more striking that usually only a few examples of the limited number of figures that were produced before 1750 are known. Many – very many – must have been lost.

The figure of Scaramouch (fig. 95) is unmarked, but a similar piece bears

95

Figurine, c. 1725-1740, h. 29 cm.

The statuette is of Scaramouch, one of the male roles in the Commedia dell'Arte, a dramatic tradition dating from the 16th century. Scaramouch is a Southern Italian with grotesque character traits, who pays court to the most beautiful women.

the mark of the owner of De Metale Pot. The model must have been made in this pottery around 1710-1720. On the grounds of the colours that have been used in it, the Rijksmuseum's example is dated to twenty years later. The Madonna (fig. 96), which is large by Delft standards, was without doubt intended for private devotions in a Roman Catholic household. It is likely that a 17th-century Madonna in wood or ivory would have been used as a model. The date 1749 refers to the year the figure was sold; the model may

96
Virgin and child, dated 1749,
h. 36 cm.

With the drape of the robe
and the slightly twisted pose,
the modeller has created an
elegant and vital Madonna
holding a lifelike baby in her
arms. The slightly purplish
blue of the decoration is
typical of the 1740s.

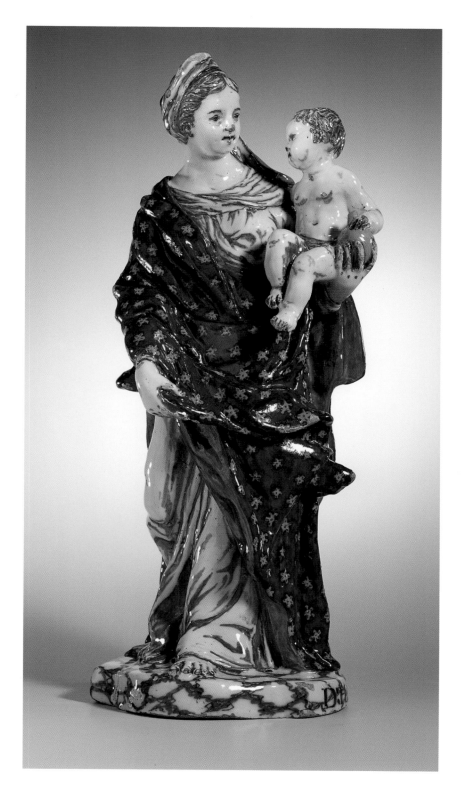

97
Plate, c. 1720-1740, attributed to De Drie Porceleyne Flessies under the management of Willem van der Kool, diam. 21.9 cm.

The design evidently caught the imagination of collectors and antique dealers. The name 'lightning pattern' plates became so common in the 19th century that it entered the trade jargon.

have stood on a shelf in the pottery for some considerable time before that. The initials DH on the side of the base are probably the initials of the customer for whom the figure was destined.

The lightning pattern, a simplified version of a Japanese *Imari* design (fig. 97), was very popular. A great many marked and unmarked plates and dishes decorated with this motif

have survived. In the past, the monogram WK was attributed to Willem Cleffius or Kleffius (d. 1679), however the potter Willem Jacobsz van der Kool fits the bill much better, given a dating of 1720-1740. This Willem, and then his widow and their son Gabriel, ran De Drie Porceleyne Flessies, a relatively small pottery in the Gasthuislaan, from 1700/1702 to 1745. There are also surviving examples with the De Paeuw mark.

98
Cup and saucer, c. 1720-1740,
h. 3.6 cm, diam. 6.7 cm (cup),
diam. 11.5 cm (saucer).

People drank tea out of small cups without handles. Millions of them must have been made in Delft, almost all of which have vanished – broken or chipped and eventually thrown away. The care with which this decoration was painted sets this cup and saucer apart from the ordinary, everyday wares.

Millions of teacups and saucers must have been made in the late 17th century and in the 18th century, almost all of which were broken in use. This example (fig. 98), beautifully painted with great care, does not seem to have been regarded as an ordinary object for everyday use by its various owners. It has survived almost as good as new. Even in difficult times, there is always a small group of the population who are very wealthy. The rich and demanding customer could insist on very high standards from the Delft potteries, as evidenced by the plaque (fig. 99) and the money box (fig. 100). The decoration on these two objects is exceptionally fine. The painter used all the colours that he had available to him in a highly functional manner. The open decoration is unusual for Delft faience – expensive pieces were often very closely decorated.

99

Plaque, c. 1725-1740, h. 36 cm, w. 32 cm.

The decoration is of great elegance with a bold use of colour. This plaque must have looked magnificent in an interior with walnut furniture.

100

Money box, c. 1725-1740, h. 30 cm.

Money boxes usually broke because of their function: after all, the coins had to be rattled and shaken out of them again once enough had been saved. The beautiful decoration on this one must have led the first owner to treat it with the utmost care.

101

Oil and vinegar set and two salt cellars, c. 1720-1735, attributed to De 3 Vergulde Astonne under the management of Zacharias Dextra, h. 16 cm (holder with jug), h. 2.8 cm, w. 7 cm (salt cellar).

The oil and vinegar set is decorated with dragons between flowers and branches, in imitation of the Chinese porcelain of this period. Objects like these were probably made to augment a service in Chinese porcelain, decorated in blue, which consisted only of plates and dishes.

102
Pair of butter dishes, c. 1735-
1755, attributed to De 3
Vergulde Astonne under the
management of Zacharias
Dextra, w. 19 cm, d. 13.5 cm
(saucer), w. 12.5 cm, d. 9.4 cm
(dish); h. 7.5 cm, diam. 11.5 cm;
h. 7 cm, diam. 11 cm.

Butter dishes were indispensable in Dutch households,
where at least one meal a day
was cold and based on bread
and butter. Like barrels, butter
tubs were originally made from
wooden staves, held together
with stripped willow, and these
shapes were copied in delftware.
The usage has now returned,
with soft margarine and spread-
able butter sold in 'tubs'.

102A
Collectors had small labels
bearing their name printed,
and these they stuck on the
bottom of objects in their
collections. The successive
owners left their marks on this
piece: L. Double, Baron de la
Villestreux, J.F. Loudon and
the Rijksmuseum.

103
Mustard pot, c. 1735-1755,
h. 10 cm.

A little tub for mustard; here
again, the modeller took his
inspiration from a wooden
cask.

104 >
Set of dishes, c. 1735-1755,
w. 11.5 cm (each).

The influence of the Meissen
porcelain factory is evident
in the colour and execution
of the decoration. After 1720,
Meissen set the trend in
European ceramics.

Zacharias Dextra bought Van der
Kloot's pottery De 3 Vergulde Astonne
in 1722. Dextra, who was a jeweller by
trade, probably thought long and hard
about what he was going to do with
the pottery, which had been renowned
for very many years. In 1726 he went
on an extended trip – perhaps on
business. Because of this he had a
deed executed by a notary, putting his
chief assistant, Adriaan van Duyn, in
charge of the pottery in his absence.
During Dextra's ownership of the
De 3 Vergulde Astonne, the pottery
developed new colours and new styles
of decoration in the enamel technique.
The modern porcelain from Meissen
in Germany was the prime example

for this. At the same time some of the
objects decorated in blue are of unpar-
alleled quality. The oil and vinegar set
(fig. 101) was previously attributed to
De Dissel on account of the D mark.
After a difficult period, this company
was bought by Adrianus Kocks in
1696 and liquidated in 1702. It seems
more likely that Dextra used a variety
of marks on the considerable diversity
of products made during the long
period that he owned De 3 Vergulde
Astonne: D, (Z:)Dex, and possibly
also V(A) (Vergulde Astonne). The
range produced by De 3 Vergulde
Astonne must have been huge. Butter
dishes (fig. 102) in various shapes and
sizes, mustard pots (fig. 103), sauce-

105

Pair of butter dishes, dated 1750, h. 6.5 cm, w. 13 cm.

The butter dishes are decorated with typical Dutch landscapes, which have in part been subordinated to the repeating, double monogram on the cover and the long side of the dish.

106

Plate, c. 1740-1755, diam. 22.5 cm.

To a significant extent, the Delft pottery owners kept their businesses going in the 1725-1750 period by producing simply decorated tableware. With these dishes and plates they competed directly with the pewter that was general in households at the time. The rhyme on this plate reveals that displacing a more expensive but also more durable product needed the occasional helping hand.

boats, sets of dishes (fig. 104), baskets and fruit dishes, many of them painted with great refinement with European images and scenes. The modeller for this company derived some of his shapes from day to day wooden utensils. The staves of wooden barrels and casks are held together by hoops of stripped willow. Lids were secured between two protruding staves. These hoops have been imitated in relief on the small oval objects. The decorations on these pieces are very similar. Although only a single butter dish is marked, everything could easily have been made in one studio. The pair of butter dishes dated 1750 (fig. 105), is so similar in shape and has such a characteristic chalk white, dry tin glaze that this set probably also came from De 3 Vergulde Astonne.

Finally, a plate with a text (fig. 106) that encourages the use of the ordinary decorated tableware:

Pewter plates are not good
Because they have to be scoured clean
But washing a plate of porcelain
Makes it clean and white again
So be sure to set the table
With a plate that's painted.

An unexpected revival and another seventy-five productive years (1750-1853)

From the political perspective, the Netherlands was not a nation of international significance during the second half of the 18th century and in the 19th century. In the mid 18th century Europe was politically unstable. The War of the Austrian Succession (1740-1748), in which France was the aggressor, was to a considerable extent played out in the Southern Netherlands, and there was great political dissatisfaction inside the country itself. In 1747, against this unsettled background, the position of stadholder was again given to a Prince of Orange, the son of William III's heir, putting an end to a Stadholderless Era that had lasted forty-five years. Although he had absolute power, William IV was an essentially weak stadholder. When he died in 1751, his three-year-old son William was much too young to succeed him in anything but name. The War of Succession was scarcely over when in 1756 most of the countries of Europe became embroiled in the Seven Years' War. The Netherlands was not involved in this war.

The economy continued to be reasonably prosperous until the period of French occupation (1795-1815), when the Netherlands was a vassal state of France. Old trade contacts and the Netherlands' position as Europe's banker generated sufficient wealth to keep the standard of living relatively high. After 1750, however, industry went into a decline, only to collapse completely in the last quarter of the 18th century. The population of the cities also decreased during this period. Amsterdam, for example, had fewer inhabitants at the end of the 18th century than it had had a century earlier. The major economic role that the Netherlands had played in European commerce and industry was now taken over by Great Britain. Rural areas, in contrast, enjoyed a new period of prosperity after 1750. Both arable and livestock farming flourished, and there were large-scale investments in agriculture. The growth of villages illustrates just how well-to-do the rural areas were during this period. Large villages like Joure and Grouw in Friesland had already developed a service function and grown into market towns. After 1750, extensive light industry flourished around them and a working population emerged to undertake all sorts of specialist work for the farming

Colour and variety, ornaments for the table and the display cabinet.

industry. The number of inhabitants rose, and with the increasing prosperity people started to assume city airs.

In Delft, too, the economic climate improved considerably in the 1750s after thirty lean years for the faience makers. Despite this upturn, the factories generally continued to tread the familiar, well-worn paths. Innovative ideas on the technical and artistic fronts that appeared elsewhere in Europe in these years appear to have caused scarcely a ripple in Delft. In 1758 the manufacturers, who were joined together in the Guild of St Luke, were concerned about the proportion of the output that was intended for the Southern Netherlands.

An increase in import duties there to protect the home industry had made export effectively impossible for the Delft potters. They made representations in Brussels and Vienna to have these duties lowered, but to no avail. Even so, no drastic measures were taken either in that year or in the next. In parts of France and Germany, the ceramics industry was virtually at a standstill because of the Seven Years' War. As imports of porcelain and faience from these areas dried up, domestic sales quite suddenly proved to have grown sufficiently to enable the Delft factories to utilize the manufacturing capacity left free by the loss of exports to Flanders. Following the relatively prosperous years for the faience industry resulting from the war, in April 1764 Delft town council issued a new 'By-law Against the Copying of the Signs or Marks of the Potteries, and the Changing of the aforesaid Signs or Marks', which was intended to prevent unfair competition. Every faience maker had to register his mark.

During the Seven Years' War a number of potteries and porcelain factories were actually set up in towns other than Delft, but none of these enterprises was to survive for very long. What is striking is that the porcelain factory in Weesp and the faience factory in Arnhem rapidly proved themselves capable of supplying products of a high technical quality and an inter-

The signboard of De Porceleyne Bijl with the mark that was registered in 1764.

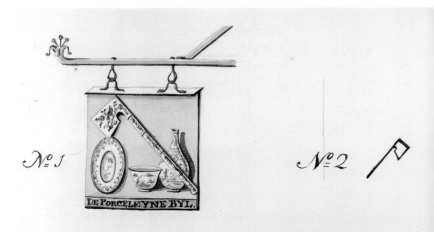

Merken Delftsch Aardewerk, na 1764

Mark	Pottery	Mark	Pottery	Mark	Pottery
A:K ★	A. Kiel "in de Witte Ster"	MP	Pieter Paree "in de Metale Pot" 1639	AP	Anth Pennis "in 't Hart" "in de twee Scheepjes"
IDM	Jacobus de Milde "in de Paauw" 1651	WVDB	Elizabeth Elling Wed v.B Briel "in t'Fortuyn" 1691	VDuijn	Johannes v. Duyn "in de porceleyne Schotel"
IDA	Johannes den Appel "in de Vergulde boot"	M	Petrus van Marum "in de Romeyn"	DeBlompot	P Verburg "in de Vergulde Blompot"
DVD (of) ❀	Dirk v.d. Does "in de Roos"	IK	Jan vd Kloot Jansz "in de Romeyn"	PD	Pieter van Doorne "in de porceleyne Fles"
(mark)	Lambertus Sanderus "in de Klauw"	G:B:S	Geertruy Verstelle "in 't oude Moriaanshooft"	DSK	Tomas Spaandonck "in de dubbelde Schenkkan"
WD	Willem v.d. Does "in de drie Klokken" heeft ook wel 3 klokjes tot merk	G:V:S	wed Jan vd Hagen "in 't jonge Moriaanhooft"	LPK	Wed Gerardus Brouwer "in de lampet kan"
A / ITD	JJ Dekstra "in de Grieksche A"	P	Justus Brouwer "in de Porceleyne Bijl"	W:V:B	Willem v. Beek "in de twe wildemans"
A / I:H	Jacobus Halder adr.24 "in de Grieksche A"	HB	Hugo Brouwer "in de 3 porceleyne Flesjes"		
	Hendrik van Hoorn "in de 3 porceleyne Astonne" (tot tot merk zijn uithangbord)	HVMD	Hendrik van Middeldijk "in t'Hart"		

The marks of the potteries till operating in 1764.

national standard of artistry. This can be explained by the large numbers of itinerant craftsmen from Germany and France, who found work and practised their trade in the Netherlands on a temporary or permanent basis.

While the export opportunities for the Delft potteries had already shrunk significantly after about 1720, the possibility of selling goods abroad appeared to have virtually vanished after the Seven Years' War. From 1765 onwards, sales on the domestic market suffered as a result of the import of newly developed English cream-ware, with modern designs at very competi-

tive prices. The factories had managed to keep afloat between 1753 (the closure of Het Gecroond Porceleyn) and 1764 (the Treaty of Rastatt), but after this the process of liquidation and merger speeded up. Seven potteries (De Vergulde Boot, De Dobbelde Schenckan, 't Hart, De Paeuw, De Romeyn, De Metale Pot and De Drie Porceleyne Flessies) were closed in the 1770s, two ('t Fortuyn and De Wildemanspoort) in the 1780s, and another three (De Porceleyne Schotel, Het Moriaenshooft – in 1773 this company, which had been split up in 1690, was back under single ownership again – and De Twee Scheepjes) before the French invasion in 1795. After about 1780 the largest and most profitable factories could no longer be sold as a whole. They became companies with twenty to forty shares, some of them owned by the heirs of former owners, some held by investors from outside the sector. The flexibility with which the pottery owners adapted to the changing market conditions during these years is remarkable. In economic terms, the twenty difficult years after the French occupation in 1795 meant the end of the industry. Another four companies were liquidated (De Porceleyne Bijl, De 3 Porseleyne (formerly Vergulde) Astonne, De Witte Starre and De Porceleyne Lampetkan). In 1815 there were just five factories left, De Grieksche A, De Blompot, De Claeuw, De 3 Klokken and De Porceleyne Fles, plus the former faience pottery De Roos, which was converted into a tile factory in 1775.

1794 saw the publication of the twelfth volume in the series *Complete Description of all the Arts, Trades, Crafts, Factories,*

Traffic, and Workshops, Tools etc. of the Same which was published by A. Blussé and Son of Dordrecht in 1788 and subsequent years. This volume dealt with *The Potter or Delft Earthenware Maker* and was written by Gerrit Paape. This little book is the only contemporary work to present a picture of the faience industry, but it was written at a time when the glory days were already more than eighty years in the past. In the introduction that precedes the chapters describing the manufacturing process, Paape sketches the rise and fall of the once so famous Delft industry. 'Of this once so flourishing Manufacture there is now, however, no more than a small and sickly remnant. Of the thirty or so Potteries that there were formerly, ten remain, almost all of them in a state heading towards ruin …

The principal causes of this regrettable decay are, assuredly, to be found in the industry of our neighbours. In various Countries people began to make similar Porcelains, among which there were some who found themselves placed in more favourable circumstances, as well as better Materials and unfairly cheaper wages, so that it is inevitable that their pieces, which were better of their kind and lower in price, are sending our Earthenware into a deep decline.' Paape was referring here not only to contemporary German porcelain and possibly to the soft paste porcelain from Tournai that had appeared on the Dutch market in the form of tableware after about 1770. He was certainly also referring to English cream-ware, which was proving a much more dangerous competitor for the Delft faience industry.

The English cream-ware industry – numerous potteries in Staffordshire and Yorkshire (Leeds) – supplied a broad spectrum of society with tableware. Technically and in terms of price, the wares produced by the Delft potteries made a poor showing against the products of their foreign competitors. We are left with the impression that no one really considered trying to develop the Delft product any further. The Delft potteries did not dare to take the step of expanding and modernizing the range. We know of no new designs for coffee and tea sets or complete dinner services dating from this period. It is also possible that the sort of consumers who wanted sets like this were tired of the relatively clumsy domestic earthenware which they knew was easily broken or damaged in use. The Delft industry was unable to deliver thin, strong tableware, hence this segment of the market was closed to the potters. They consequently focused on a prosperous rural community that was satisfied with sets of plates and dishes that would seldom have been subjected to any sort of intensive household use. But Paape also had a tale of woe to tell when it came to the aesthetic aspect. 'Here in this country, in contrast, because people usually seemed more eager to make money than to see to it that the Arts and Sciences achieved the highest possible level of perfection, the zeal to continue to add all the greatly praised beauties to the Pottery began to noticeably diminish; little by little it thus became less in inward value as in outward appearance.' At that point there was, in fact, only one way of saving the Delft industry from ruin: the introduction of the English technique of making cream-ware with a body that was white through and through. At the end of the

18th century, some of the factories did make the switch, perhaps also encouraged by a competition organized by the *Oeconomische tak van de Hollandsche Maatschappije der Weetenschappen* (Dutch Society for Trade and Industry). This institution promised premiums for wares that could stand up to comparison with English cream-ware. It seems likely that De Porceleyne Fles, acquired by Henricus A. Piccardt in 1804, De Grieksche A, allied to the firm of Leij, Bellaard & Co from 1812 onwards, and De Blompot, absorbed into the firm of Terburg, Perk & Co in 1813, produced primarily 'English' cream-ware. Two potteries remained loyal to the old technology: De Claeuw, the firm of Sanderus & Co as of 1806, and De 3 Klokken, the firm of Jacobus van Putten & Co from 1809 onwards – they made nothing but tin glazed earthenware.

The fortunes of the potteries in the first half of the 19th century were dictated by economic crises and political changes. After the company that had taken over De Grieksche A went into liquidation in 1818, the four remaining factories continued to produce on a modest scale. Little is known about these companies' domestic sales. De Porceleyne Fles manufactured not only 'English' cream-ware with a completely white body covered with a transparent lead glaze, but also oven-proof stoneware for bakers. With these two products, the company was ultimately to emerge as the sole survivor of the wave of liquidations. The 19th-century product manufactured by De Porceleyne Fles no longer bore any relation whatsoever to the original Delft tin-glaze pottery.

The two factories that continued to manufacture according to the old techniques, De Claeuw and De 3 Klokken, must have been relatively small businesses. De Claeuw was a company with twenty, later sixteen shares, De 3 Klokken had forty. A number of shareholders had 'portions' in both firms. These two companies suffered in the crises of 1839-1843. In September 1840 'Willem Hendrik van der Mandele, broker, Jacobus van Putten, private citizen, and Jacob Kuyzer, merchant, presently the sole remaining shareholders in the existing Company, De 3 Klokken Pottery in Delft, acting as the firm of J. van Putten & Compagnie' bought De Claeuw for seven thousand guilders. In the following year, the operations of De 3 Klokken were transferred to De Claeuw's premises and the site and buildings of the former pottery, De 3 Klokken, were sold for eleven thousand guilders to the Kingdom of the Netherlands, which used them to expand the state warehouses. The worsening economic outlook and the chance to sell the land and buildings of one of the two companies must have been the reason for this merger. The period of prosperity that followed the economic upturn in 1843 was short-lived. In 1849 Jacobus van Putten & Co of De 3 Klokken was still an enthusiastic exhibitor at the national industrial exhibition in Delft. But at some time in 1851-1852 the last two partners decided to liquidate the company, and they put the buildings up for auction in August 1853. The buyer chose not to avail himself of the opportunity to buy the movable plant and equipment. After two hundred and thirty years, the curtain finally came down on the Delft faience industry.

We owe our knowledge of the number of potteries still operating in the 1760s and the marks used in Delft in the second half of the 18th century to measures taken by the Delft town council in 1764. The renewal of the rule that the wares had to be given a mark meant that a very great deal of material dating from the period after 1765 is marked and can be attributed to a specific factory. No single faience manufacturer and its products emerge as obviously dominant during this period. We can, though, see differences between the ten or so successful companies and the nondescript second-raters. By 1780 the majority of this latter group had closed down.

In 1759 Zacharias Dextra, who had owned De 3 Vergulde Astonne since 1722, sold his flourishing business to Hendrik van Hoorn. To help the young Van Hoorn find his feet, Dextra continued to run the company's technical operations for the next few years; he died in 1762. Van Hoorn revealed himself as a businessman with a keen sense of the mood of the times. Objects bearing the Van Hoorn mark (VH or 3 astonne) are usually good quality (figs. 128, 129).

Zacharias's nephew, Jan Teunis Dextra, married the daughter of his uncle's next-door neighbours, Catharina van der Kool. After the death of her mother in 1757, she acquired De Grieksche A from the estate by buying out the shares of the other heirs. Jan Teunis must have known the trade from top to bottom, but he does not seem to have been much of a businessman. The company was sold in 1764, and he officially remained the chief assistant under the next owners.

Two enterprising women, Geertruy Verstelle and Elisabeth Elling – the widow Van den Briel – were prominent during this period. They saw the opportunity to make a success of Het Oude Moriaenshooft and 't Fortuyn respectively in the 1760s. These must have been extremely productive companies, both of which also made tableware in contemporary designs. There is a relatively large amount of good material dating from these years that bears the mark of one of these two potteries.

Between 1740 and 1785 two generations of the Brouwer family, Justus and his son Hugo, managed the relatively small and previously not very successful pottery known as De Porceleyne Bijl. They managed to build this company up into a highly productive business which made a great many plates and dishes, garnitures (ornamental vase and jar sets) and tableware.

In this period the pieces with the most sophisticated design and the finest decoration came from De Porceleyne Schotel and De Twee Scheepjes, which had their premises not far from each other in Molslaan. Jan Pennis had bought De Porceleyne Schotel as far back as 1724 and steered it through the difficult times of the 1730s and 1740s, before buying De Twee Scheepjes in 1750. It is not impossible that this company was actually intended for his son Anthonij. In 1764 Jan sold his first company to Johannes van Duijn. Anthonij, his wife Rachel and their son Jan Pennis Junior were actively involved in De Twee Scheepjes until 1789. Johannes van Duijn was probably the grandson of the Adriaan who had been the chief assistant at De 3 Vergulde Astonne.

A great many marked pieces from the potteries that continued manufactur-

107

Dish, c. 1750-1775, diam. 36 cm.

What a variety of things the pottery had for sale: fish strainers, milk jugs, plates and dishes and above all ornaments. The Dutch interior was crammed with porcelain and faience; if it were up to the Delft manufacturers, it would of course be Delft faience. A dish like this gave the shopkeeper and the customer new ideas.

ing until into the 19th century have survived. The long production period, coupled with the late date when the objects were made, means that vast quantities of simple plates and dishes, garnitures and tobacco jars have survived. They are marked with a 'claw', 'three bells' or LPK, the mark registered for De Porceleyne Lampetkan in 1764.

The best work dates from the first fifteen years of the period covered by this chapter. Judging by the quality of the marked objects, it was after this that the decline in the design, execution and decoration of the standard output set in. There are however exceptions to this general observation – a number of extraordinary pieces that sometimes bear a person's name and often a date. Technically and artistically, the faience makers continued to be capable of great achievements for a very long time, but the opportunities for making and selling outstanding objects were steadily eroded over the years as their market dwindled.

The dish (fig. 107) may possibly have been made as an advertisement, a piece to be displayed in a pottery's sales outlet or in a shop to show all the things needed in a house, particularly in terms of china: a set of ornamental vases to display on top of a cupboard, a rack and plates, a fish strainer, milk jugs, a brush back and all sorts of decorative items like plaques on the wall, dishes on a little shelf, bowls large and small on a cabinet. As well as the china there is an auger, a dustpan and brush, a cake tin, a folding table, a cradle, a window washer, a ladder, a nappy dryer, a cupboard and a child's chair, a kettle on a

108
Dish, c. 1750-1775,
diam. 35.5 cm.

Chinese women repose in a
garden setting. The dish is not
intended for use on the table, it
is a decorative piece to be hung
on the wall.

109
Dish, c. 1750-1775, diam. 35 cm.

The Bible with its edifying
stories played an important role
in the everyday lives of Dutch
households. A few appealing
stories depicted on delftware
were an educational element in
the home.

110

Dish, c. 1750-1775, diam. 35 cm.

The pastel shades of the decoration are typical of the 1760s.

111

Dish, c. 1750-1775, diam. 35 cm.

A daring design: rarely did a Delft painter paint just a branch, without a border around it and placed asymmetrically in the space.

112
Cockerel, c. 1750-1775, h. 20 cm.

The cockerel looks at us jauntily. His Chinese counterpart arrived in Europe in unpainted white, and was painted cold with oil paint. The Delft potteries could do it better in faience: the colours shine out.

burner and a selection of baskets. A cat and a dog, real or painted, complete the contents of the Dutch domestic interior.

These four objects (figs. 108, 109, 110, 111) are a selection taken from a large group of dishes in the museum's own collection and elsewhere that were made specifically as decorative objects and were never intended to be used at table. The superb and diverse decorations are typical of the years around 1760. The Chinese women (fig. 108) sit and stand in a garden-like setting enclosed by a screen. This design may well already have been in use for a generation by this time; the use of light shades in the painting indicates a date after 1750. The Last Supper (fig. 109)

was undoubtedly painted after a print in a series that the company had in stock for use when an order was placed for a dish with a biblical scene. The border is extremely successful – the colourful foliage makes a magnificent foil for the rather stiff picture. The curling tendrils (fig. 110) likewise form a strong contrast with the open river landscape. This dish has an unmistakable Rococo feel. The origin of the sprig of wild blossom (fig. 111) lies in the Far East. Without this influence, no Delft faience painter would ever have dared to place the decoration thus.

Changes in the interior design of homes, other eating habits, a new fashion – these were all aspects of life that the faience manufacturers in Delft had to take into account. Possibly following the German example, which set the trends in the porcelain industry, in the third quarter of the 18th century, the Delft potters started to make huge numbers of figures and figurines of varying sizes. Occasionally the modelling is clumsy and awkward, but the best examples surpass the figures produced at the beginning of the century in quality and execution. The great majority of these objects were intended as ornaments to be displayed in glass cabinets or on étagères. The brightly coloured Delft faience evidently found a ready market in the Netherlands, customers for whom the German porcelain was too expensive or perhaps too refined. A number of factories must have been producing an enormous output. These four examples (figs. 112, 113, 114, 115) are a selection from a varied group in the Rijksmuseum's collection. The cockerel was made after an exam-

113
Pair of horses jumping a fence,
c. 1765-1785, h. 24 cm.

Two dressage horses captured
at the moment of their jump.
They are among the most
popular Delft creations.

ple in Chinese porcelain, the so-called
blanc de chine, which was purchased unpainted from provincial kilns in one of
the coastal provinces and was painted
cold with oil paints in Europe. This
technique was sometimes also used on

white Delft figures, but both types lack
the gloss and the bright coloration of
pieces with the decoration in the glaze.
The two dressage horses captured at
the instant of their jump are among the
most popular of the Delft creations.

114
Pair of shoes, c. 1750-1775,
l. 13 cm.

There is little similarity between
these little shoes and the example in figure 14 (p. 40), but then
they are separated by a hundred
years of fashion and a hundred
years of technical developments.
It is their colour that is the most
striking feature.

model from De Porceleyne Bijl, the company that Justus Brouwer had successfully built up. The larger European porcelain factories employed full-time designers, who usually also had to make the moulds. In a very few cases they were actually skilled sculptors, but the modellers also frequently worked from examples, such as existing small pieces of statuary, or from prints. This design may be derived from a statue by Pieter Xaverij, who modelled a great many genre groups in Leiden shortly after 1670. Much of his work was still in Dutch collections in the 18th century. In Delft, De Metale Pot and De Witte Starre did employ carvers as modellers for a while (see also pp. 97-99 and 142), but this was exceptional.

How bright and cheerful a well-laid table must have looked in the third quarter of the 18th century. The Delft faience makers produced all sorts of novelty pieces in the form of fruit painted in natural colours that could be set out on the table. A great many of these objects have survived. An arrangement of apples, pears, bunches of grapes and a plum is shown here as an example of what they could do (fig. 116). Tureens in the shape of birds, such as ducks and lapwings, and animals, like goats and sheep, are often found in small sizes, which suggests that they were used for small snacks. They may also have been used for pies or similar dishes, with each diner getting an individual tureen by his plate. These small tureens are typical of what the Delft factories were producing. They were manufactured in such a tremendous variety that they were probably made in a considerable number of potteries. These models were

115

Bagpiper, c. 1760-1785, attributed to De Porceleyne Bijl under the management of Justus Brouwer, h. 27 cm.

There must have been a three-dimensional example; the designers in Delft very seldom came up with a figure of their own.

Two of these imposing beasts often formed the nucleus of a collection of Delft figures. And no collection would be complete without pairs of miniature shoes. This phenomenon recurs in every period in Delft (see also p. 40, fig. 14), but never before had they been produced in such colourful variety as in the 1750s and 1760s. The bagpiper, almost thirty centimetres tall, is a

116
ruit, c. 1750-1775, l. 12 cm
pear and apple), l. 10 cm
plum), l. 14.5 cm (grapes),
. 12 cm (pears).

Small items to decorate the
able at any time of the year.

designed for large-scale production-line manufacture, and the different elements, such as stands and bases, were interchangeable. The little Delft tureens consist of a stand and a separate base with a cover on which the animal, bird etc. sits. In the case of tureens in the shape of fruit, the base and the cover together sometimes imitate the whole fruit. This melon

on a stand (fig. 117) is a fine and very well preserved example made by De Porceleyne Bijl.

In Strasbourg, the leading centre of European faience manufacture in the mid 18th century, they took the *trompe l'oeil* effects further by modelling a whole animal, perhaps placed on a realistic base. The animals were painted on the glaze in their natural colours in the

accurately. Rather than resting on a base, this creature is supported by its legs, so that it is raised above the base and the underside could thus also be glazed. As was usual in Delft, the whole thing was painted in *grand feu* colours.

The figures of men and women sitting on barrels or on rocks, which could be filled with liquor, are evidence of exceptional craftsmanship. They are fitted with a small spigot so that the contents can be drawn off into a glass. This figure of a man (fig. 119), almost sixty centimetres tall, is one of the most spectacular examples of this genre. The pose of the figure is an indication that such objects were usually supplied as sets: man and wife face each other. Small jugs in the shape of monkeys sitting on rocks must have been part of the standard range at many of the potteries. A great many have survived, displaying all sorts of minor variations. This example (fig. 120) wears

117
Tureen, c. 1760-1775, attributed to De Porceleyne Bijl under the management of Justus Brouwer, h. 16 cm, diam. 19 cm.

A melon on a stand. The bottom section has a foot ring that fits into the well of the stand like a cup and saucer. The top section acts as a lid.

petit feu technique. When the modellers in Delft worked from an example like this from Strasbourg, such as this tureen in the shape of a duck (fig. 118), they copied the shape more or less

118
Tureen, c. 1760-1775, h. 28.5 cm.

Rather than resting on a base or among reeds, this duck stands on its legs and one other support. The bird looks as though it could waddle off at any moment.

119
Liquor jar, c. 1760-1775,
h. 56.5 cm.

The separate head is the stop-
per, like the cork in a bottle.
Filled with wine, or perhaps
something stronger, this will
have been the centrepiece of a
festive gathering.

a tricorne hat with a removable crown. The inscription tells us what it was used for: *kees is goet – hij geeft melk in overvloet – als je sijn buik maar vol doet* ('Kees is good – he gives plenty of milk – just so long as you fill his belly'). In 1759 Zacharias Dextra sold his company, De 3 Vergulde Astonne, to Hendrik van Hoorn. In the deed, Dextra explicitly stipulated that he was to keep the 'fine enamelled' pieces

to trade in on his own account. We do not know how much longer Van Hoorn went on producing white wares that were painted on the glaze. The specialist painters are unlikely to have all left at once when the business changed hands, and Dextra remained in charge of the technical management of the factory for several years. It is not clear whether objects like the wall fountain, the tureen and the basket

120
Milk jug, c. 1760-1780,
h. 19.5 cm.

A novelty item that was evidently very popular; a great many milk-pouring monkeys have survived with various appropriate legends.

121

Wall fountain with basin,
c. 1750-1770, h. 42 cm,
w. 26.5 cm (fountain),
w. 39.5 cm (basin).

In the painted cartouches
around the landscape one
can discern the first signs
of the Rococo. The model
must already have been old-
fashioned at the moment
when it was painted.

121A

The collector John F. Loudon
regarded the part of his collection of Delft faience with the
decoration applied on the glaze
is very important. An etching
of the best piece was included in
the catalogue of the collection
that Loudon had published in
1877.

(figs. 121, 122, 123) were made in this
factory or another one. Delft also had
several independent workshops where
the white wares were painted on the
glaze. The decoration could be fired
on to the glaze at about 600 degrees
Celsius in a relatively small enamelling
kiln.

The wall fountain (fig. 121) is one of
the largest and most beautifully decorated pieces in this technique. In the
cartouches we can detect the first signs
of the Rococo, a style that filtered
through to Delft late and was used
on only a modest scale. The tureen
(fig. 122) is modelled on a piece of

122
Tureen, c. 1760-1770, h. 29.5 cm,
w. 44 cm.

The Delft designer took his
inspiration from a German
porcelain tureen. One must,
however, wonder just how
strong and, more importantly,
heat resistant a piece like this
was in faience as compared
with the version in porcelain.
Time after time, advertisements
insisted that a particular type
of earthenware or porcelain
would not crack even if boiling
water were poured into the
object. Evidently this was by
no means always the case.

German porcelain. This large piece
is decorated with flowers and with a
coastal view in cartouches. The basket
(fig. 123) was certainly decorated in the
same studio. The shape of the basket
echoes the silver bread baskets that
were being made in Amsterdam and
The Hague around 1750. The scal-
loped edge, the imaginatively modelled
handles and the sides with the incised
half-rosettes can easily be envisaged
in silver. The basket is the very latest
fashion in shape and decoration, something that was quite unusual for the
Delft faience industry in this period.

This model must have been extremely
popular. There are five in the Rijksmuseum alone that are more or less
the same shape but have very different
decoration (see also fig. 126).
With the next two objects, marks do
give us something to go on for attribution to a factory. But even here the two
manufacturers, Anthonij Pennis of De
Twee Scheepjes and Jacobus Halder,
who was the owner of De Grieksche A
between 1764 and 1768, may well have
entrusted the painting to a specialist.
This inkstand (fig. 124), the tureen
and the basket are all painted in bright

123
Basket, c. 1760-1770, h. 12.5 cm, w. 33.5 cm.

The decoration is executed in bright colours, which to modern eyes have a rather harsh look, with sharp contrasts.

colours. The *petit feu* technique that was used means that the colours did not fuse into the white glaze, and this gives them a rather hard, sharply contrasting look. In the evening, however,

when rooms were lit only by candle-light, these pieces would have come into their own and shown up well. These two goblets and the vase with covers (fig. 125) were probably part of a set of five or possibly even seven goblets and vases. The modeller seems to have had fun playing with the three dimensions.

The goblets have an unusually low centre of gravity with undulating lines in the height and the width. The foot and the bottom and top of the goblets and the vase are built up entirely of rocailles. The covers resemble short-ened Chinese robes that drape over the edges. The female Chinese heads poke jauntily out of the top.

This basket (fig. 126) is identical in shape to the basket with polychrome decoration (fig. 123). The basket is

124
Inkstand, c. 1765-1775, h. 21 cm, w. 19 cm, d. 8.5 cm (holder), w. 24 cm, d. 15 cm (stand).

The inkstand unites four functions that were essential in a study of the period: light, somewhere to put a timepiece, and holders for ink and 'pounce' to scatter over freshly-written text in order to dry the ink.

125
Set of vases, c. 1765-1770,
attributed to De Grieksche A
under the management of
Jacobus Halder, h. 42 cm.

In this set of vases the free
undulations of the Rococo are
combined with chinoiserie
decorations. This model must
have been so *à la mode* that it
also rapidly fell out of favour
and disappeared from the
range, since no other set with
matching covers is known.

126
Basket, c. 1758-1765, attributed
to De Grieksche A under the
management of Jan Teunis
Dextra, h. 13 cm, w. 31 cm,
d. 23.3 cm.

The decoration on the basket is
more than a century old: the
base is decorated with a water
landscape after examples of early
17th-century Chinese porcelain.

marked with the initials of Jan Teunis
Dextra, who owned De Grieksche A
until 1764. Another example in the
Rijksmuseum, with a contemporary
decoration, bears the mark of Jacobus
de Milde, owner of De Paeuw until
1768. We might infer from this that
commercially desirable items were

freely copied. Another possibility is
that one pottery helped out another by
letting it have baskets in the form of
semi-manufactures; the other factory
could then glaze the pieces, decorate
them and fire them again. The loca-
tions of the potteries involved here
would tend to support the second
thesis: De Grieksche A and De 3 Vergulde Astonne were next door to each
other, De Paeuw less than a hundred
yards away from the other two.
When Geertruy Verstelle found herself in a position to buy the once so
renowned company, Het Oude
Moriaenshooft, in the autumn of 1761,
she must have had a very good sense
of the opportunities of the moment
and picked up the reins with drive
and enthusiasm as soon as she took
control. With the kettle on a burner
(fig. 127) she marketed a product that
was very much of its time. It is evident

127
Kettle on a burner, c. 1760-
1770, attributed to Het Oude
Moriaenshooft under the management of Geertruy Verstelle,
h. 23 cm, w. 33 cm (kettle),
h. 10 cm (burner).

The painting partly echoes the
decoration in relief; a landscape
is painted on the body of the
kettle. The figure has an inkwell
next to him and an eagle at his
feet; everyone at this period
would have known that he represented St John the evangelist.

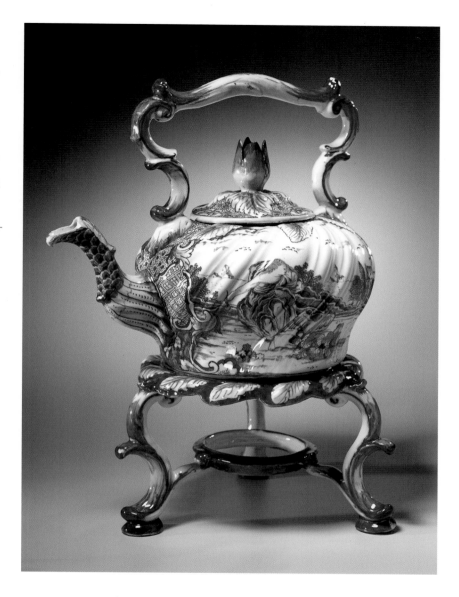

from the number which have survived
that this set was successful. The designer probably took as his model a kettle
on a burner made of silver or pewter.
This is typical of the style of kettle that
was being produced in silver in the
1750s and 1760s, both in Amsterdam
and in The Hague. Just how practical
a faience kettle would have been to keep
the water for the tea hot is debatable,

but there can be no doubt that this
large piece was fragile. We cannot rule
out the possibility that it was purely
ornamental.

Hendrik van Hoorn owned and managed De 3 Vergulde Astonne (later
De 3 Porseleyne Astonne) for forty-
five years. In the early days he probably
continued along the lines set out by the
previous owner, Zacharias Dextra, who

128

Tureen, c. 1760-1770, attributed
to De 3 Porseleyne Astonne
under the management
of Hendrik van Hoorn,
h. 32 cm, w. 38 cm.

The cover of the tureen is in the
shape of a Chinese hat, topped
with an elegantly turned curl,
shaped and painted to look like
a pumpkin stalk.

129

Hyacinth container, c. 1770-1780,
attributed to De 3 Porseleyne
Astonne under the manage-
ment of Hendrik van Hoorn,
h. 15.5 cm, w. 27.5 cm.

The hyacinth suddenly became
very popular as a flowering
houseplant. At first, existing
objects like flower holders were
adapted to this new use, but
it was not long before special
models were designed for the
purpose. They had a grid with
several large round holes to hold
the bulbs and a number of smaller ones in which to put sticks
to support the flowers and add
water to top up the container.
It is quite remarkable that this
grid should have survived, given
the inevitably rough handling it
must have undergone when the
bulb was cut out.

assisted him in running the company
for some years after the sale. After this
he undoubtedly set about expanding
the range according to his own tastes
and ideas. This tureen (fig. 128) was

copied from a model made in the
German town of Höchst. The shape
was so popular around 1750 that many
of the faience manufacturers in Europe
copied it. This model was also made in

130
Set of vases, c. 1740-1760, attributed to De 3 Vergulde Astonne under the management of Zacharias Dextra, h. 27 cm.

The beakers and vases are decorated with an open landscape with a Chinese figure. This is a standard set of good quality with good decoration of the kind that was produced from about 1725 until the end of the 18th century.

Chinese porcelain as a special order. With his entrepreneur's hat on, Van Hoorn apparently also saw opportunities in the liquidation sales of other firms. On 3 February 1774, the liquidation of Van Kerckhoff's faience pottery in Arnhem was advertised: 'Be it hereby known that on Monday the 21st day of February 1774, in the City of Arnhem, the Auctioneer Gillis van de Wall of said city will be selling to the highest bidder at a public sale a large quantity of MOULDS and MODELS, as well as other tools belonging to a Faience Factory'. Van Hoorn seized the chance to enlarge his company's range: he bought some or possibly all of the moulds and models that had been designed in Arnhem around 1760 by one or more designers from the Strasbourg area, at that time the most modern that were available in the Netherlands. The hyacinth container (fig. 129) was originally one of these

Arnhem models. Around 1750 it had been discovered that it was not necessary to grow hyacinth and daffodil bulbs for the interior in pots and earth, and that they could be brought into flower very effectively on a sort of grid over a bowl of water. In the third quarter of the 18th century hyacinths became extremely popular as flowering house plants, and so special containers were designed for the purpose. This piece had originally been intended for a very fashion-conscious clientele. This is something of a contrast to the general picture in Delft in the 1770s, where the factories produced luxury items for a rather more provincial section of society. Van Hoorn must have been very well aware that the moulds he bought in 1774 were rather old-fashioned after fifteen years. But this was what his customers wanted. Throughout the 18th century, sets of vases and jars (fig. 130) were an extreme-

131
Punch bowl, c. 1750-1775,
diam. 33 cm.

In the 18th century people in the
Netherlands started to emulate
the English and drink punch,
an alcoholic beverage served
hot in a large bowl. This piece
is decorated with a group of
people drinking punch after an
engraving by William Hogarth.
On the other side a gentleman
is served with a glass that is so
hot the steam rises from it.

ly popular decorative element in the
Dutch domestic interior. They were the
usual ornaments that graced the tops
of the typical Dutch cabinets and china
cupboards. The shapes and the decoration did to some extent follow the
fashion of the moment, but popular
models remained in production for
many years. This set is a very common
size and shape. The quality of the
finish is good and each of the beaker
vases has its original cover. Each piece
is marked 'D' and '6'. In the past this
mark was thought to have been used
by De Dissel, but it is now attributed
to Zacharias Dextra in De 3 Vergulde

Astonne. Judging from the shade of
blue, this set was most probably made
around the middle of the century.
Large bowls (fig. 131) were often used
as ornaments and displayed on cabinets, but in this case the decoration
would indicate that this piece was actually intended for use in the home. This
punch bowl has no cover and it would
appear that it never did have one. It is
therefore difficult to say whether this
elegant piece was meant to be used or
was just an ornament.
Fish strainers (fig. 132) were part of the
standard equipment of a Dutch household in the 17th and 18th centuries.
This practical utensil was usually made
of lead-glaze earthenware or undecorated faience. This example, like the
set of vases (fig. 130), is decorated
with a Chinese figure in a landscape.
Herring dishes (fig. 133) are also typical of the Dutch kitchen. They are
often shaped like a fish; in this case
it is an elongated dish decorated
with a painting of a herring.

132
Fish strainer, c. 1740-1780,
diam. 49.8 cm.

Boiled fish was drained on a
strainer. The customary decoration on this indispensable
Dutch household utensil is a
few fishes or a formal pattern,
which meant that the perforations were not a problem. It is
possible that this particular
piece was intended solely as
an ornament in an elegantly
appointed kitchen.

133
Herring dish, c. 1760-1790,
attributed to De Porceleyne Bijl
under the management of
Justus Brouwer or his heirs,
w. 22 cm, d. 13.5 cm.

Gutted and salted, but still
raw, herring is a typical Dutch
delicacy that many foreigners
find hard to stomach. Needless
to say, every house had a special
dish for serving it.

34

Plaque, c. 1750-1775, h. 55 cm,
w. 44 cm.

The Delft painter was really at a
loss as to what to do with the
large area so he reduced it by
painting an ornamental border
round the central scene, in
which he placed small medallions containing familiar scenes
of shepherds and shepherdesses,
and farmers sowing seeds. For
the main picture, a scene from
the story of the Prodigal Son
(Luke 15:11-32), the painter used
a new print, just published by
J.G. Hertel of Augsburg. This
model assured him of figures in
contemporary dress.

In the second half of the 18th century
the production of plaques, 'porcelain
paintings', flourished as never before.
The great majority are relatively small
objects with a frame in relief, in which
there was a hole for hanging them.
The decoration varied in quality and
subject. Biblical stories, domestic
scenes, landscapes, chinoiseries and
often a vase or basket of flowers in
bright colours generally meant that
these plaques and plaquettes were
cheerful little works. Here, too, the
Rijksmuseum has a fine collection,
although it lacks the more simply
decorated examples, which are much
more common. The potteries used
saggars with a maximum of barely fifty
centimetres; their production process
was based on this. For a large piece like
this plaque (fig. 134) a special support
had to be rigged up in the kiln, using

fireproof material wedged between the
saggars.
The plaquette with a landscape painted
in blue (fig. 135) seems at first glance to
be a drawing in a plain dark varnished
wooden frame. This frame, however,
like the picture itself, is delftware and
is of a piece with the surface. The illu-
sion of the simple wooden frame in
conjunction with the picture after a
17th-century example led an earlier
generation of art historians to believe
that this plaque must therefore date
from the 17th century. Increased
insights into the use of the different
shades of blue during two centuries
of manufacturing in Delft and the
knowledge that in the third quarter of
the 18th century artists and craftsmen
frequently drew inspiration from 17th-
century examples mean that this piece
is now dated a hundred years later. The

135

Plaque, c. 1750-1775, h. 16 cm,
w. 19.5 cm.

The finely painted landscape on
this plaque is after an etching
by Jan de Visscher, made after
a drawing by Jan van Goyen
dating from the third quarter
of the 17th century.

187

136
Plaque, c. 1750-1775, h. 32 cm, w. 24 cm.

This plaque with its bouquet of two tulips has been one of the most popular pieces of faience in the Rijksmuseum ever since it was acquired in 1911.

137
Plaque, c. 1770-1790, h. 32 cm, w. 35 cm.

One can easily imagine the scrolls of the border being carved in limewood. In clay, too, it was a contemporary surround that is entirely in keeping with the choppy seas it frames.

same applies to the particularly finely decorated plaque (fig. 136). The painter has captured the colourful posy with two tulips extraordinarily well. This plaque, which has no border, would originally have been mounted in a dark wooden frame. Contrary to the Delft tradition, the little seascape (fig. 137) has no painted cartouche inside the border. The piece as a whole is a successful imitation of a seascape in oils with a finely carved frame.

The Rijksmuseum's collection includes a great many occasional pieces, objects that were made to order in one of the Delft factories, often for a specific per-

138
Plate, dated 1753,
diam. 24.7 cm.

The barge owner D. Rees
carried Delft faience to
Amsterdam. It seems likely
that Rees ordered these plates
as goodwill gifts to present
to his customers. Obviously
a gift of this kind would be
dated.

138A
In the second half of the
18th century the profile of
the standard plate changed.
It stood on a rim around
a concave bottom.

son. These pieces seldom have a factory mark but they are usually dated. In
consequence we do not know where,
but we do know when the object was
made. As a rule they are meticulously
decorated with subjects that had something to do with the profession of the
person giving or receiving the gift.

On the well of this plate (fig. 138) we
see the barge of one D. Rees, who
called himself 'Carrier of Delft Porcelain to Amsterdam'. Rees, born
in Delft in 1707, operated out of his
birthplace. He died in the town in
1769. Behind the towpath with two
walkers can be seen the skyline of
Delft with the Nieuwe Kerk, the town
hall and the Oude Kerk. The vessel's
deck cargo consists of baskets that are
undoubtedly packed with faience.
There are several other surviving examples of this plate, some of which bear
the monogram of Hugo Brouwer or
of his father Justus. It seems likely that
the Brouwers, father and son, made
these plates for Rees to hand out to
his customers. After about 1750, plates
with a diameter of twenty to about
twenty-five centimetres have a charac-
teristically heavy profile; the foot ring

139
Cream pot, dated 23 September 1767, h. 21.2 cm, w. 29.9 cm.

Thanks to the skill of the potter, the various elements make up a single piece with good proportions. The shape of the cover with knop, which has – most unusually – survived, was taken from an example in wood.

140
Puzzle jug, dated 1768, h. 25 cm.

A gift for a special occasion, a joke for a man of rather traditional tastes who in 1768 deserved an attractive, but already somewhat dated present.

underneath has disappeared and has been replaced by a sort of hollow. The border is wider in relation to the well than in previous years. Brouwer used ordinary plates from the current stock for Rees's order.

The shape of the pot (fig. 139) means that the cream floats on top of the milk in a thick layer, and the milk can be poured off through the straight spout set low on the body. The model was not specific to one particular Delft pottery. Cream separators made in coarse earthenware, covered with lead glaze, had existed since about 1650. The potter in the factory would have used one of these as his example. The decoration of the piece, made up of different 'pictures', leads us to suspect that cream pots were not part of the pottery's usual repertoire. The rural scenes on the wall and the cover point to the function of the cream pot, but must also have reflected the daily life

41
Tobacco jar, dated 1769,
h. 16.5 cm, w. 18 cm.

The little man holds a roll of
Brazilian tobacco on his lap.
This is how tobacco leaves were
shipped to the Netherlands.
This *pirouette*, as it was called,
was often used as the shop
sign for tobacconists in the
18th century.

41A
The inner cover of the
tobacco jar.

of the recipient, Jan Janse Tetteroo, who received this object as a gift on 23 September 1767.

For this special occasion, the date of the puzzle jug (fig. 140) was incorporated into the openwork decoration.

The belly of the jug is decorated with a water landscape and beautifully detailed swags of foliage and sprigs of flowers. The top, perhaps to make the holes less obvious, is marbled in a dark tone, and the painter has accentuated the excised leaf motifs in a deeper shade of blue. The scale of the landscape, the greyish blue in a few nuances and the elegance of the decoration are typical of the period up to 1770. It is possible that puzzle jugs were already outmoded by this time, but one more was made in 1768 for a special event. Elegant tobacco jars were often made of silver in the Netherlands. The shapes of the versions in pewter and faience were derived from the silver models. The decoration of this example (fig. 141) of 1769 consists of completely filled borders, and cartouches containing scenes of rural life, including peat-workers stacking peat. The extent of the decoration and the careful

142
Advertising plate, c. 1760-1780,
h. 24.7 cm, w. 33 cm.

Hendrik Rusing was apparently
what we would nowadays call an
importer and wholesaler: he sold
all sorts of Delft (domestic) and
English (imported) earthenware,
which he sold to the trade but
also, if it suited the merchant,
retail.

finish are indications that a generous
budget was agreed when the piece was
commissioned. The little man who
serves as the knop on the cover has a
roll of Brazilian tobacco on his lap.
Most unusually, the inner cover has
survived. This goes down as the stock
shrinks. An additional cover like this
helps to stop the tobacco from drying
out. The text emphasizes once more
the function of this object. On the
underside of the jar are the initials of
the first owner and the year in which
he received the jar: A.D.W. and 1769.

The tray (fig. 142) that was decorated
for Hendrik Rusing marks the end
of the last boom period in Delft. It
appears to be a contemporary form
of advertising; it could perhaps be an
object that would now be regarded as
window dressing material. The text
sums up the reason for the decline in
the industry in a few succinct words.
The faience from Delft had to share
its market with the technically much
better English wares.
The surviving objects from the last
quarter of the 18th century reveal just

143

Plate, c. 1770-1800, attributed
to De Porceleyne Bijl,
diam. 23 cm.

This goes back to a design made
hundred and fifty years before.
Evidently there was still a
demand for traditional decorations like this, despite the age
of the pattern.

how accurate Paape was when he wrote about the mediocre standard of artistry at this time. The products dating from this period lack almost any form of artistic invention or innovation. They are often simply a recycling of old models and decorations. The technical quality also deteriorated slowly but surely, although this may have been caused not so much by lack of skill as by the fact that the potteries were serving a different class of customer and by the resultant need to keep the cost price down. This plate (fig. 143), which is twenty-three centimetres in diameter, shows how the next genera-tion of Brouwers at De Porceleyne Bijl resorted in the 1780s to repeating an object that had been made a hundred and fifty years earlier. The style of the painting, the use of colour and the decoration of the border are a faithful copy of a majolica dish of about 1630 (see also figs. 1, 2). However, the potter simply used a standard plate from the current output rather than specifically making a dish after the original. The plate with the portrait of stadholder William V (fig. 144) comes from the same factory. A great many plates with portraits of this Prince of Orange, his wife, Princess Wilhelmina of Prussia, and their children have survived. Plates were also produced with all sorts of loyal mottoes emphasizing the people's devotion to the House of Orange. This 'Orange ware', probably displayed on edge in a very old-fashioned man-

144

Plate, c. 1780-1790, attributed
to De Porceleyne Bijl,
diam. 23 cm.

Plates with portraits of the
stadholder, his wife and their
children were very popular at the
end of the 18th century. On the
eve of the French Revolution,
the conflict between various
political factions in the Netherlands boosted sales of wares like
this. Orange trees and mottoes
like *Pray For Your Sovereign* left
no doubt as to the owner's
political persuasion.

145

Preaching engagement plate,
c. 1788-1800, diam. 22.5 cm.

Drawing lots using a roulette
wheel but with no profit motive
might be another way to
describe this highly unusual
object. The six ministers listed
mounted the pulpits of the two
large churches in Delft without
any rota, entirely as chance
determined.

146
Dish, dated 1789, diam. 34.3 cm.

The closer one was to the source, the easier it was to arrange for a special present. Occasional pieces, like this wedding dish, were very often ordered by or for people who actually lived in Delft. Cornelis van der Hoeven and Geertruij de Bruijn lived in the town when they got married and remained there for the rest of their lives.

ner, decorated the rooms of the large middle class.

Three late occasional pieces (figs. 145, 146 and 147) testify to considerable technical and artistic quality. At the end of the 18th century, the Reformed Church in Delft employed six permanent ministers for the Oude Kerk and the Nieuwe Kerk. There were two sermons every Sunday and also evening services on various days during the week. The preachers did not take to the pulpit in turn, in accordance with a fixed rota, but set the place and time with the aid of a preaching engagement plate, a wheel made specifically

for the purpose. The names of the six ministers are written on the star-shaped spinning top: from Petrus Hugenholtz, appointed in 1766, to Diderik van Rossem who arrived in 1788, the last of the men to come to Delft. They continued to hold these posts in this combination until 1805. This preaching engagement plate must have been made soon after 1788. Even now everyone immediately understands the significance of the symbol on the base of the dish (fig. 146). At the moment of their marriage, on 23 August 1789, the hearts of Cornelis van der Hoeven and Geertruij de

147
Dish, c. 1790-1820, diam. 36 cm.

The text expresses the utmost contempt for lawyers.

The Farmer
I live an Upright Life

The mariner
Straight or crooked
So Long as I Have it
I Don't Care

The Lawyer
I can make Crooked Straight
And so I wear a Robe of Scarlet
Red

The Devil
You Could Turn from Crooked to
Straight
But I'm a Tougher Nut to Crack

148
Dish, c. 1770-1810, attributed to De Porceleyne Lampetkan, diam. 34 cm.

This design, generally referred to as 'peacock's tail' by collectors and dealers, looks more like a bunch of dried flowers with a few feathers incorporated in it.

196

149
Dish, c. 1800-1840,
diam. 34.8 cm.

These brightly coloured dishes
were originally made for simple
country people, but nowadays
grace the lavish kitchens of
many a large house in the
Netherlands.

Bruijn were forged together for ever.
They married in the Oude Kerk in
Delft, Van der Hoeven as a widower.
They continued to live in Delft, where
Geertruij died after almost twenty-
four years of marriage. The border is
set off with yellow, now worn, a subtle
finish to the dish that was very popular
at this time. The flower decoration on
the border, partly in the reserve technique where the background is painted
and the design is left white, must have
been exceptionally labour-intensive
and expensive, particularly for this
period. Nevertheless, the execution
of the border lacks the elegance of
the borders of the first half of the
18th century.
Could the conduct of lawyers, not
infrequently a sore point, have stirred
up so much emotion around 1800 that

there was thought to be a market for
this striking dish (fig. 147), or did one
person, dissatisfied with his lawyer's
behaviour, have it made specially? The
text reveals intense contempt for the
legal profession. The piece is rather
crudely made. The colour of the 'Robe
of Scarlet Red' is rather pale and even
slightly washed-out. The other colours
are harsh. Amusing as it may be, the
painter of this piece, which dates to
around 1800, was certainly no great
master of his craft.
A wide range of dishes with full decoration was made for a well-to-do rural
population. The 'peacock's tail' motif
is one that must have been produced in
large numbers and by several different
factories. This dish (fig. 148) is marked
LPKan, for De Porceleyne Lampetkan, which went into liquidation in

150

Set of vases, c. 1820-1850,
attributed to De 3 Klokken
under the management of
J. van Putten & Compagnie,
h. 45.7 cm (jar), h. 32 cm
(beaker).

In producing these pieces,
De 3 Klokken pottery was
attempting to equal the standard
of the early 18th century. In
terms of quality of design and
decoration, they were successful.
The treatment of the original
Imari style betrays the fact that
this set was made in a later
period: the Biedermeier era.

1811. These brightly coloured dishes
(fig. 149) may not have been made
until after the turn of the century.

The output of the last surviving potteries to work traditionally, De Claeuw
and De 3 Klokken, probably consisted
primarily of repetitions of these sorts
of dishes, plates and holloware – sets
of vases or garnitures, apothecary jars
and tobacco jars – after 18th-century
models and with hand-painted decorations, sometimes slightly modernized.

The prosperous bourgeoisie got its
tableware chiefly from Germany and
Great Britain. English-style cream-
ware made from clay that fired white
was also produced in Luxembourg and
Northern France. It is by no means
impossible that many families in this
precarious period in Dutch history did
not buy anything new, but simply used
the 18th-century tableware that must
have been present in abundance in
most households. The products of the
last Delft potteries still producing were

not intended for the well-to-do. The factory owners must have long since abandoned any ambitions in that direction. There was just one exception – Jacobus van Putten, who as manager and co-owner of De 3 Klokken tried to equal the best pieces from the 18th century under his own name, J. van Putten & Co. The garniture (fig. 150) decorated in *Imari* style is a good example of this. It must have been made around 1840, a period when Van Putten was still submit-

ting his best pieces for industrial exhibitions. Less than thirty years old, this set was already described as 'antique' by about 1870, when it was part of the John F. Loudon collection. His heirs gave the pieces to the Rijksmuseum in 1916, when they were put on display in the galleries.

The Phoenix rises from the ashes

'Seldom could one see such a wealth of Delft earthenware together as at the Delft Exhibition, and among the pieces the finest examples, outstanding in the refinement of the drawing, in the freshness of the colour, in the superiority of the glaze, and in the beauty or whimsicality of design. The imitation of the Japanese or Chinese porcelain, the masterly designs on some of the tiles, plates and dishes, everything deserved the admiration of the thousands of visitors. Some of them displayed a single figure, or a few flowers, or a simple landscape, in swiftly drawn blue outlines with a few flat shadows. Others, in contrast, were worked up in more detail, and revealed an endeavour to emulate the works of the great masters in colouration and effect.'

This quotation, a commentary to an illustration of two *petit feu* painted butter dishes in the collection of reproductions that appeared after the closing of the great historical exhibition that was staged in Delft in 1863, very clearly expresses the enthusiasm for and the considerable appreciation of Delft faience that existed in the Netherlands at that time.

A mere ten years after the closure of the last traditional pottery, a general historical interest in old objects stimulated a few people, some of them in the Netherlands, to take a closer look at Delft earthenware.

The first edition of the *Guide de l'Amateur de Faïences et Porcelaines* had appeared as early as 1861. A second edition was published in 1863, followed by a number of reprints in the course of the century. This book grew from a modest guide numbering only 176 pages into a substantial work with more than 1500 pages, almost 100 of which were occupied by the chapter dealing with Dutch delftware. Auguste Demmin, the author of this book, was undoubtedly inspired by the latent interest he discerned, but he was also to guide the collecting of Dutch delftware as a result of his works. Evidently there was already an interest in this product on the part of private French collectors by the end of the 1850s, and Demmin responded to this for the first time, in 1861, by writing at length about Delft faience. We may censure him for making the whole field appear older and, above all,

For his traditionally-minded clientele Van Putten made exceptional ornamental sets that went well in a 19th-century interior.

> (pp. 202-203)
The display at the historic exhibition in Delft in the summer of 1863.

201

more beautiful than it actually was, but his exaggerations gave the interest in Delft its momentum.

One of the collectors in the Netherlands to respond virtually immediately was a Frenchman, Charles Antoine Edouard, Baron de la Villestreux. In 1861, at the age of thirty, he was appointed second secretary at the French embassy in The Hague. It must have been at the Delft exhibition, to which he lent a 'fine copper chandelier with a number of branches', that De la Villestreux was captivated by Delft faience. Given his modest and non-ceramic loan to the exhibition, it seems unlikely that he already had a collection of delftware in 1863. In the four or five years that followed, however, in part using the Delft exhibition, he succeeded in amassing a superb collection, which must have consisted of more than 250 objects. In 1867 or 1868, but in any event before May 1869, the good Baron sold the major part of his collection, or possibly even all of it, to John Francis Loudon.

Loudon was born in Rotterdam on 21 May 1821. He followed in his father's footsteps and operated as a merchant in the East Indies. In 1850 Loudon, on leave in the Netherlands, became involved in the plans to explore for tin on the island of Billiton in the Indonesian archipelago. After a shaky start, the business boomed, and Loudon had a considerable holding in it. After eighteen years he retired from the company and settled in The Hague, where he lived off his investments. He decided to collect, and looked for an appropriate field: he found Delft faience. He must have sensed the feverish interest in delftware that had suddenly gripped col-

lectors and tackled this, for him, new activity in a typically businesslike manner: he acquired 250 first-class pieces by buying De la Villestreux's collection in its entirety. He then went on to buy whatever he could get and, in principle, at any price. Simply building up this fine collection was evidently not enough to satisfy Loudon though; by publishing a catalogue in 1877 he let everyone know what he had. To do the job, he employed the Frenchman Henri Havard, who had compiled the catalogue of the Van Romondt decorative arts collection in Utrecht in 1875. In the space of seven – at most eight – years, Loudon had seen the opportunity to put together the most important collection of delftware and at the same time, by publishing this catalogue, of giving this product, a focus of national interest, a firmer footing.

The following year saw the publication of the *Histoire de la Faïence de Delft*, also by Henri Havard. Given Havard's in-depth archive research and his work on compiling the catalogue of Loudon's collection as a warm-up exercise, we may safely regard this as the first substantial and well-researched guide to the subject.

At present we only know about the important collectors, the ones who stood out from the rest in terms of the quantity and quality of their collections, because these are the only people who are mentioned in the contemporary literature and it is only their collections – or at least their sale catalogues – that still exist. But below this exalted level there must have been a sizable group of more minor collectors; old Delft must really have been in fashion, otherwise it is impossible to explain the manufacturers' interest in starting to produce faience in the old style. In his description of the fine and applied art at the Paris World Fair in 1878, Henri Havard celebrated the revival of the French faience industry in jubilant words. 'It was almost a scandal when thirty or so years ago a few stalwart connoisseurs, who called themselves artists, started to admire old earthenware and boldly declared that the beauty of forms took precedence over the fineness of the material. It was a close-run thing – these lovers of old pots and pans were almost considered to be mad. We can now recall these disputes calmly… The consequences that crowned their efforts are too fine, too great, too complete for them to have any reason to complain. The old earthenware has risen again like the Phoenix from the ashes. All the old shapes can be found at the 1878 exhibition… Quimper is producing imitation Rouen ware and at Dèvres they are continuing the art of Nevers. M Montagnon of Nevers even made a Rouen dish of such extraordinary dimensions that Louis Poterat, were he to return to this world, would have been astounded. The potters of Delft, so proud of their porcelain violins, would be beaten now by a double bass.' Two factories in the Netherlands – De Porceleyne Fles in Delft and De Gebroeders Tichelaar in Makkum – followed suit with these imitations before 1880. On the wave of growing appreciation and status it was worthwhile making new 'old' delftware industrially in the Netherlands too. In 1887 De Porceleyne Fles was given a superb collection of antique Delft by King William III, and in consequence this earthenware became the national

decorative art product *par excellence* around 1890 – indeed, it was perhaps even considered as being part of the Dutch identity. The Dutch, after all, are no strangers to chauvinism.

And so it is that the Delft product, which was manufactured for 230 years with varying degrees of success, became a much sought-after subject of collection and study in Europe and beyond.

Inventory numbers and provenance of the principal pieces

Inventory numbers

1	BK-NM-7990
2	BK-16008
3	BK-1983-24
4	BK-NM-14190
5	BK-NM-3983
6	BK-1958-33
7	BK-1999-92
8	BK-NM-8242
9	BK-NM-5733
10	BK-NM-3895/3896
11	BK-NM-4804
12	BK-2002-11
13	BK-14976
14	BK-1957-11
15	BK-NM-12400-42
16	BK-NM-12400-3
17	BK-NM-12400-2
18	BK-NM-3133
19	BK-NM-12400-79
20	NG-KOG-1711
21	BK-NM-11856
22	BK-NM-12400-7
23	BK-NM-12400-9
24	BK-NM-476
25	BK-15312
26	BK-NM-3310
27	BK-NM-12400-43
28	BK-NM-12400-35/38/39/40
29	BK-1961-45
30	BK-1962-62-A
31	BK-16535
32	BK-NM-12400-445
33	BK-KOG-2422
34	BK-1986-16
35	BK-1959-37
36	BK-1983-16
37	BK-1981-4
38	BK-1975-73
39	BK-1969-107
40	BK-1958-22
41	BK-1958-26
42	BK-1980-31
43	BK-1962-54
44	BK-1963-30
45	BK-1957-26
46	BK-1960-171
47	BK-1955-64
48	BK-1998-44
49	BK-1962-60
50	BK-KOG-1533/1534
51	BK-NM-12400-91
52	BK-NM-12400-93
53	BK-NM-11096
54	BK-14852
55	BK-NM-12400-109
56	BK-1969-31
57	BK-16536
58	BK-KOG-1536
59	BK-1993-4
60	BK-NM-12106
61	BK-NM-11467
62	BK-NM-12400-211
63	BK-NM-12400-214
64	BK-1961-98
65	BK-1959-54
66	BK-1989-18
67	BK-NM-12400-209/210
68	BK-1957-22
69	BK-NM-11746
70	BK-17317
71	BK-NM-12400-265
72	BK-NM-12400-323
73	BK-16104
74	BK-NM-12400-332
75	BK-1963-45
76	BK-NM-12404
77	BK-NM-12400-278
78	BK-NM-11399
79	BK-17318
80	BK-NM-12400-286
81	BK-NM-12400-329/330
82	BK-NM-12400-338/339
83	BK-1959-79
84	BK-NM-12400-362/363
85	BK-NM-12400-403/404
86	BK-1958-34-B
87	BK-NM-12400-425
88	BK-1963-44
89	BK-15575
90	BK-NM-12400-54
91	BK-NM-12400-486
92	BK-NM-12400-95
93	BK-NM-12400-100
94	BK-NM-13318
95	BK-16393
96	BK-1973-207
97	BK-NM-11631
98	BK-1961-38
99	BK-1955-66
100	BK-NM-12400-230
101	BK-1961-32/33
102	BK-15313, BK-NM-12400-406, BK-NM-12400-408

Provenance

Gift of Mrs Adriana Maria Aronson-
Stigter, 1989
   37, 66
Gift of A. Bredius, 1886
   8
Gift of Mr & Mrs Carp-Henny, 1948
   73
Gift of J.E. van Heemskerck van Beest, 1877
   5
E. van Hoboken Bequest, 1925
   94, 132, 139, 148-149
On permanent loan from the Royal
Antiquarian Society
   20, 33, 50, 58, 135, 145
Gift of the heirs of John F. Loudon, 1916
   15-17, 19, 22-23, 25, 27-28, 32, 51-52, 55,
   62-63, 67, 71-72, 74, 77, 80-82, 84-87,
   90-93, 100, 102-105, 107-115, 116 (2),
   118-123, 125, 129-131, 134, 137, 141, 147,
   150
Gift of a friend of the museum on the
occasion of the 40th anniversary of Queen
Wilhelmina's reign, 1938
   116 (1, 3, 4)
Gift of A.W.M. Mensing, 1916
   76
Gift of J.C.P.R. Menso, 1944
   89
Gift of E. de Neufville, 1885
   1
Gift of W. Vogelsang, 1906
   106
Gift of P. and G.A. Voûte, 1937
   13

Delffse Porceleyne is a publication of the
Rijksmuseum in Amsterdam and Waanders
Publishers in Zwolle. Several ceramics experts
provided a critical commentary on the text.

Translation
Lynne Richards, Seaford (England)

Photography
Department of Photography Rijksmuseum
– Jeroen Kho and Monique Vermeulen – and
other institutions mentioned in the captions,
to which the following should be added:
p. 10 Philadelphia Museum of Art: given by
Mrs Gordon A. Hardwick and Mrs W. Newbold
Ely in memory of Mr and Mrs Roland L. Taylor;
pp. 32, 162, 163 and the map on the back jacket
flap Photoreproduction Gemeentearchief Delft
(original copyright reserved); p. 37 Historisches
Museum Frankfurt am Main, photo: Margit
Matthews; p. 45, fig. 17A Rijksdienst voor
de Monumentenzorg, Zeist; p. 65 photo:
W. Hoekstra-Klein, Delft; p. 81 Nelahozeves
(Czech Republic), Nelahozeves Castle,
The Lobkowicz Collections

Design
Berry Slok bNO, Hilversum

Printing
Waanders Printers, Zwolle

ISBN 90 400 8831 4
NUR 655

For more information on the activities of the
Rijksmuseum and Waanders Publishers, please
visit www.rijksmuseum.nl and www.waanders.nl